Somerset Villages

Following page
Muchelney. Situated on a slight rise above the Levels, the 'great island'
of its name, which brought Benedictine monks here to this peaceful
place in the late 7th or early 8th century.
In front of the Perpendicular church of SS Peter and Paul are the
excavated abbey remains. There survives the Abbot's Lodging (left), a
fine and very complete rebuild within 50 years prior to the abbey's
dissolution in 1538, together with the outbuildings of the
farm into which it was converted.

Somerset Villages

ROBIN BUSH

Photographs by Julian Comrie

THE DOVECOTE PRESS

Old Farm Cottage, Clapton-in-Gordano.

First published in 1995 by the Dovecote Press Ltd
Stanbridge, Wimborne, Dorset BH21 4JD

ISBN 1 874336 35 0

Text © Robin Bush 1995
Photographs © Julian Comrie 1995

Designed by Humphrey Stone

Photoset in Sabon by The Typesetting Bureau, Wimborne, Dorset
Printed and bound in Singapore

British Library Cataloguing-in-Publication Data
A Catalogue record of this book is
available from the British Library

1 3 5 7 9 10 8 6 4 2

Contents

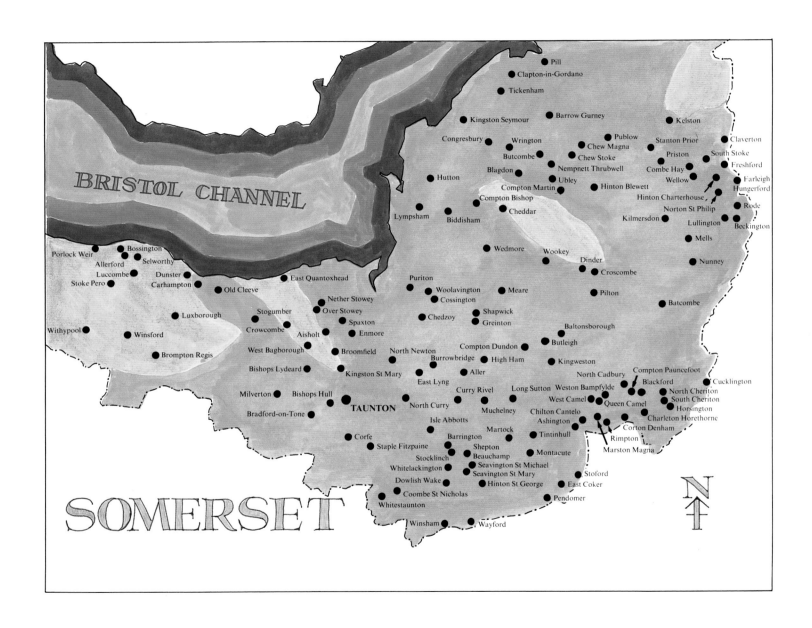

Somerset Villages

Now the light falls
Across the open field, leaving the deep lane
Shuttered with branches, dark in the afternoon,
Where you lean against a bank while a van passes,
And the deep lane insists on the direction
Into the village,

T.S. ELIOT *Four Quartets: East Coker*

What makes a village? There was a time when, asked to list the necessary ingredients, the proverbial man or woman in the street would stipulate a church, chapel, school, shop, and pub. Today, under the impact of very different economic circumstances, several of the villages included here have lost all these features apart from the church. In some cases even the church will have been declared redundant and most villages now share their Anglican minister with their neighbours, swallowed up by streamlined team ministries. In small places with depleted populations, even a few parish churches are now family homes, as at East Cranmore and Wheathill. What remains is still a village but the quality of its life has changed. There are fewer opportunities for villagers to meet, gossip and set the world to rights: important opportunities in a beautiful county like Somerset where the second home is becoming increasingly popular with the affluent city dweller. And yet there are still some corners of Somerset where the lord of the manor lives in the home occupied by his ancestors, where the village shop and post office provide personal contacts unavailable at the distant hypermarket, where the old inn daily houses the local debating society, and where fund raising still relies on the village fête with a brass band playing on the green.

But then change has always been part of the village story. Take a village like Long Sutton. Only 80 years ago it still had its own blacksmith, dress maker, cutler, baker, chimney sweep, coal dealer, butcher, haulier, stationer (with Post Office), shopkeeper, insurance agent, grocer, two beer retailers (as well as the Devonshire Arms) and two wheelwrights (one of whom also worked as a carpenter, builder and undertaker). Go back a further 80 years and the majority of such villages were largely self-sufficient in goods and services, supplemented by periodic visits on market day to towns like Taunton, Yeovil or Wincanton. Go back before this and you enter a semi-feudal world where the man in the big house often owned the whole village and controlled the very lives of most of its inhabitants. A world which may have been free of income tax, council tax and VAT but in which the villager would be subject to highway rates, poor rates, church rates, hearth tax, window tax, land tax, tithes, lay subsidies, reliefs, heriots, and other long-forgotten customary dues. A world of backbreaking work, deprivation, disease, superstition, long-established tradition and the parish workhouse: the only available consolations – cider, ale and religion. A world in which petty larceny could warrant a public hanging and serious crimes could mean gibbeting at a major crossroads or on a remote hill: the body supported by an iron framework long after it had decomposed, to act as an object lesson to all those who passed by. Perhaps change *has* after all been for the best.

The wonderfully-varied landscape of Somerset – hills, valleys, moors, woodlands, marshes, green and rolling pastures, lush and fertile fields – has given birth to an equal variety of settlements. The different soils and rocks have provided a wide range of building materials, from golden Hamstone and blue Lias to Mendip limestone, Quantock sandstone and the humble cob. Most of our villages are recorded at least as far back as the Domesday Book of 1086 and, had the documents survived, many could probably be shown to have their origins as far back as the 7th century when the Saxons first conquered and assimilated the Romano-British people: the harried survivors of a dying empire. In some cases there are Prehistoric and Roman sites quite close to later villages, although demonstrating continuity of settlement is usually impossible. The location of the church, often cheek-by-jowl with the principal manor-house, will usually indicate the earliest area of Saxon settlement. Occasionally the parish church will be isolated from the later village, suggesting that for various reasons the physical (and possibly economic) focus of the community has shifted. There are villages which line a single street or focus on a particular road junction; those which centre on an open space or village green and those which comprise more than one early estate, leading to the development of secondary hamlets. Sometimes, generally on higher ground, settlement was dispersed throughout parishes, often on ancient farm sites where there had never been many houses or farms in the vicinity of the parish church. In lowland areas village expansion was often restricted by the medieval open arable fields, divided into furlongs and strips, which virtually surrounded some villages, in which most of the farmhouses were situated.

Many villages still bear the names of those Saxons who founded them, although we know nothing of their individual lives: Mærec at Marksbury, Deor at Durston, Luca at Lufton, Spak at Spaxton, Bealdhun at Baltonsborough and Cuthwulf at Cothelstone. These must have been the men whose eyes first lighted on a fertile valley, a strategic river crossing or a sheltered bay and decided to make them their homes. It is tempting to interpret these names as those of individual farmers establishing individual farms which acted as the nuclei of the later villages. In cases where the place-name includes the personal name and the element *ingas* ('the men or people of ...') we can possibly infer that the village was founded or taken over by a group or extended family headed by the named person. Examples of this would be Wihtlac's people at Whitelackington, Cusa's people at Cossington, Bara's people at Barrington, Cucola's people at Cucklington and Lulla's people at Lullington. Other villages which had common Saxon or British geographical names such as Combe or Stoke often added the suffix of their Norman lords' surnames to distinguish them from each other: the Beauchamps at Hatch Beauchamp, the Mallets at Curry Mallet, the Dandos at Compton Dando, the Cantilupes at Chilton Cantelo, the Plugenets at Haselbury Plucknett and the Haweys at Combe Hay.

Much scholarly attention has been paid in recent decades to villages which have been abandoned at different periods. Some of these never seem to have recovered from the Black Death of 1348-9: places such as Little Marston in West Camel, Speckington in Yeovilton and Nether Adber in Mudford. Others were deliberately swept away by lords of the manor who wanted to empark the areas round their grand houses and found that the villages they owned were in the way or spoilt the view – Cricket St Thomas, Kingweston or Nettlecombe. At Farleigh Hungerford the village was probably relocated in the 15th century to allow for the expansion of the castle there. In a very few cases some places died because the industry on which they depended failed – hence the 'ghost' village of Brendon Hill, deserted after iron-mining there ceased in 1883.

Most of the places included here headed 'ancient' parishes with their own parish churches, but a few developed from small hamlets which grew up in the shadow of older, more extensive villages, such as Allerford and Bossington in Selworthy, North Newton in North Petherton, Stoford in Barwick and Pill in Easton-in-Gordano. At the other end of the scale, some villages almost became towns in the 12th or 13th centuries, exploited by their lords as the sites of planted boroughs: Norton St Philip, Crowcombe, Chew Magna, Nether Stowey. Others, like Dunster or Milverton, did indeed become successful towns but, with the decline of their markets or manufacturing, are now regarded as villages again.

Inevitably the more picturesque aspects of most villages are illustrated here but, although parish churches figure prominently, other rural focuses are depicted: pubs, village greens and manor-houses. Somerset has a rich heritage of vernacular buildings, the study of whose architecture and history has considerably advanced in recent years, and included here will be found as delightful a collection of small appealing flower-framed cottages as anywhere in the country.

To make a representative selection from so many delightful settlements has not been an easy task and apologies are offered to all those whose own personal or favourite spots have been omitted. An attempt has been made to illustrate many places not included in our previous colour volume – *Somerset, A Portrait in Colour* (1989). The imminent extinction of the luckless hybrid county of Avon is celebrated by returning to the old pre-1974 county boundaries for this volume. Fuller accounts of most villages included here will be found in my *Somerset, the Complete Guide* (1994), to which readers are also referred for some account of sources used in preparing the text.

Finally, this book is rightly a *visual* celebration of the Somerset village: the third book on which I have worked in partnership with my friend and photographer, Julian Comrie. Once again he has amply demonstrated his genius for depicting our county in all weathers and in all seasons, its wonderful range of textures and its splendid landscapes.

ROBIN BUSH
Taunton

AISHOLT Viewed from above, this small village is almost hidden in the Holcombe valley high up on the Quantock Hills: its cottages lining the lane which winds down the slope below the church of All Saints. There were two estates here in 1086, Holt (the later Aisholt) and Holcombe, which together passed in the late 14th century to the Fichets of Spaxton and later their heirs, the Hills. In addition to farming there was quarrying, limeburning, tanning and, for a few years from 1714, copper mining. The poet Sir Henry Newbolt, author of the celebrated poem 'Drake's Drum' and buried at Orchardleigh in the east of the county in 1938, spent most of his later years at the Old School House here.

ALLER The original Levels settlement, possibly a small Saxon religious house, stood on Aller 'island' in the vicinity of the church of St Andrew, here pictured at sunset, and the adjoining Aller Court Farm, formerly the manor house. Here in 878 King Alfred brought the Danish King Guthrum for baptism after the victorious Battle of Edington in Wiltshire and, following the nearby Ciivil War Battle of Langport in 1645, Sir Thomas Fairfax spent the night in the village before continuing on to Bridgwater after pursuing royalist troops through the parish. The surrounding 'moors' or marshes were inclosed by Glastonbury Abbey in 1234, although the lord, Ralph of Aller, attempted to prevent this by bribing the abbey's steward with 'a most noble cockerel'.

The later village developed around the junction of three lanes, shown in our second picture, before expanding north and south along the lower slopes of Aller Hill. The Pound Inn, formerly the White Lion, was first built on the roadside waste in 1571, and takes its present name from its proximity to the manor pound. The Parish Council bought the lordship of the manor in 1910 in order to secure this pound as the site for a telephone box!

ALLERFORD The classic Somerset view of packhorse bridge, adjoining chimneyed cottage and Packhorse Inn, without which no book on the county's villages would be complete. Allerford (the 'alder ford') was a civil tithing but lay within the parish of Selworthy and seldom seems to have had a single lord after the 11th century. In Domesday (1086) there were two manors here, both held by Edric under Ralph de Limesi, also lord of Selworthy, but each had its own mill and each, as in Saxon times, rendered twelve sheep a year to the royal manor of Carhampton.

ASHINGTON The Early English church of St Vincent with its sizeable bellcot instead of the more usual western tower: a feature also used to good effect at Chilthorne Domer and Brympton D'Evercy. The stone balustrades flank the entrance to Manor Farm, almost hidden by trees and set back from the quiet road between Limington and Mudford, although the eastern part of the 15th century building was sadly swept away in the 19th century. The name, 'Essentone' in Domesday, seemingly derives from its situation to the east of the old county town of Ilchester – although south-east would be nearer the mark. Few of my

acquaintances have ever heard of Ashington, let alone visited it, but I love its air of peace, its attractive white fencing and village pond, in what anywhere else would be a mundane flat setting. It must have been a wrench for the St Barbe lords of the manor when in 1605 they acquired Broadlands in Hampshire (later home to Earl Mountbatten) and moved away from Somerset.

BALTONSBOROUGH The 15th century church of St Dunstan, a chapelry of Butleigh until 1895, with an elaborate weathervane topping its west tower. The dedication almost certainly identifies the village as the birthplace of Dunstan in about 909, as it is known that he was born 'near Glastonbury', which is only five miles away. Dunstan was educated at Glastonbury Abbey, rose to become its abbot and then Archbishop of Canterbury, before inspiring the revival of monasticism throughout England following the Viking raids. He also crowned King Edgar at Bath in 973 and devised the coronation service which has formed the basis of all subsequent English coronations. Baltonsborough itself had been given to Glastonbury in 744 by Lulla, a 'handmaid of Christ', and was probably administered for the abbey by Dunstan's father, Heorstan, nephew of the first bishop of Wells and later reeve of all the abbey's estates. A sexist epitaph of 1784 proclaimed:

Praise to my wife is justly due,
I've proved this maxim to be true,
The richest portion with a wife
Is obedience and a virtuous life.

BARRINGTON Contrasting domestic views of this lovely Hamstone village north-east from Ilminster. It was a place visited by King John in 1207 but today most tourists come to see Barrington Court and its wonderful gardens – a stately home built away from the village to the north-east by William Clifton, a wealthy London merchant who had bought the manor on the attainder of Sir Thomas Arundell in 1552. The Duke of Monmouth was entertained there on his western progress of 1680 by William Strode, whose family were noted Parliamentarians during Cromwell's Commonwealth. It was perhaps the Strode influence which led at least ten villagers to join Monmouth's ill-fated rebellion in 1685. The village lies mainly along a single street in which stands the church of St Mary, dating from the 13th century, the Royal Oak, formerly the Victoria Inn, and the so-called Priory.

BARROW GURNEY A peaceful domestic group under a dramatic sky south-west from Long Ashton. To Barrow (*bearu* – 'grove' or 'wood') was added 'Gurney' to mark its ownership by the Gournays, lords of the manor in the 13th century. One of the family had founded a nunnery here by 1212, the site of which after its dissolution in 1536 became the estate of Barrow Minchen (*mynecen* – 'nun') centred on Barrow Court. The two manors were united in the 1680s by the alleged kidnapping of 13-year-old Ruth Tibbott, heiress to Barrow Gurney, and her forced marriage to William Gore of Barrow Court, after her own mother had failed to sell her to the highest bidder. The deaths of an engaged couple here in 1704, Samuel Heal and Jane Hunt, were commemorated in a verse epitaph:

> *Here lie we, both bereaved of life,*
> *Who thought to have been husband*
>   *and wife.*
> *'Twas grim faced death that brought us*
>   *hither,*
> *We lived in love and lie together.*

BATCOMBE The striking and finely detailed 87 feet west tower of the church of St Mary, built between 1539 and 1543, that stands prominently above the valley which named the place. The tower was probably one of the last projects engineered by the abbots of Glastonbury, who held both manor and church from the 10th century, passing after the dissolution of the abbey to the Bisse family of nearby Spargrove. In the early 17th century Bishop Laud ordered his chaplain to whitewash out a quotation from Isaiah in the church which he deemed 'a Jewish piece of scripture'. The Puritanical flavour of the parish, at odds with the medieval richness of the church, was fostered by the Bisses and led to an unsuccessful raid on Bruton by 'the raging Batcombites' in 1642 during the Civil War. A choice epitaph of 1847, recorded here, states:

It was so suddenly I fell,
My neighbours started at my knell,
Amazed that I should be no more,
The man they'd seen the day before.

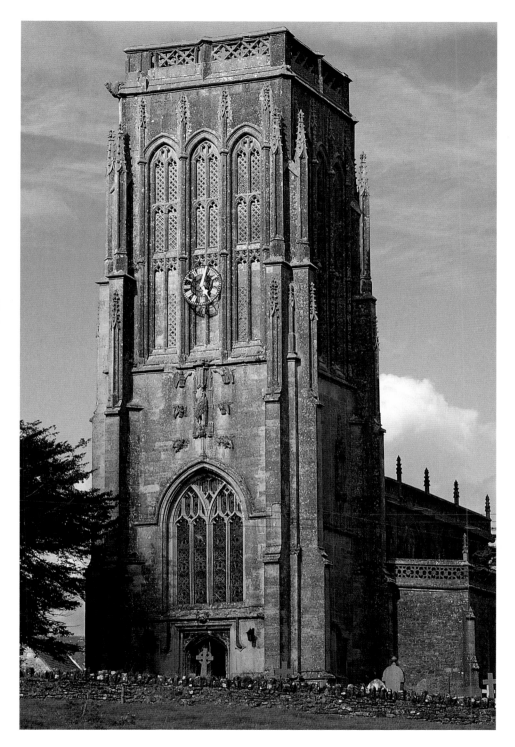

BECKINGTON A side street dappled in sunlight in this former cloth-producing village to the north-east of Frome. It is a place of fine stone houses, several of them substantial, such as Seymour's Court, the Abbey and Beckington Castle. The church of St George is not only notable for having the best Norman tower in Somerset but for the religious crisis of 1635 when the churchwardens with the support of the parishioners refused to move the altar from the body of the chancel, like a dining table, to the east end of the chancel at the order of Bishop Piers. The churchwardens were twice excommunicated, imprisoned and in 1637 finally forced to do public penance in the churches of Beckington and Frome, and in Bath Abbey. At Beckington Turnpike in September 1766, after Somerset MP, Thomas Prowse, had failed in his efforts to pacify starving rioters, an eight-hour gun battle ensued when they vainly tried to storm the mill.

BIDDISHAM The Perpendicular church of St John the Baptist with its eccentric tower: tilted towards the west but stabilised with a modern top stage. It contains a Norman scalloped font and Jacobean pulpit. The small village developed along a lane running north from the A38 between East Brent and Lower Weare, later spawning settlement along the main road. The estate was held by Wells Cathedral from Saxon times: its income used from the 12th century to repair and furnish that building, while the vicarage supported the cathedral schoolmaster. If an early forged charter of 1065 is to be believed, the Celtic name of the place was Tarnock, formerly 'Ternuc', possibly meaning 'winding stream'. This name was borne by two manors in the Domesday Book (1086), both held by the lord of Bridgwater, Walter of Douai, and today refers to a nearby scatter of houses.

BISHOPS HULL The centre of this hilltop village immediately west of Taunton which, as Hulle, formed one of the divisions of the great manor of Taunton Deane. This estate was owned by the bishops of Winchester from Saxon times – hence the prefix of the village's name. The church of SS Peter and Paul has a 13th century tower, probably built by the monks of Taunton Priory, but the body of the building was largely rebuilt in 1826-7. Inside, however, are some excellent benchends and fine monuments to the Farewell family, builders in 1586 of the nearby so-called Manor House. The village was home to Amos Fish, 'a superannuated exciseman', who died in 1764. 'He was a man who had acquired some knowledge in the sciences and often electrified himself, for which purpose he had two machines, each different in degree of operation, which he found of great use to rouse his decayed faculties.'

BISHOPS LYDEARD Set against a backdrop of the Quantock Hills, the village is almost hidden among trees. Only the magnificent 15th century tower of the parish church and Lydeard House are clearly visible, the latter built c.1750 for John Coles, a local lawyer. The 'bishop' in the place's name recalls the grant of the manor by King Edward the Elder, son of King Alfred, to Bishop Asser of Sherborne, later passing to the bishops of Wells when the cathedral was established in 909. The village itself, a popular home for Taunton commuters, retains at its heart several thatched cottages in the local red sandstone, almshouses founded in 1616 by Sir Richard Grobham, and a satisfying number of atmospheric inns. At one of these, the Lethbridge Arms (formerly the Gore Inn) one of the last cudgel-playing matches in Somerset was staged in 1836. In the mid 19th century it was claimed that a poor man here was troubled by the devil whenever he passed a particular place. He arranged for a clergyman and two masons to accompany him and, when the devil appeared again, the minister ordered him to depart while the masons surrounded him with a hastily-built wall. The evil one was never seen again !

BLACKFORD Set amid lush fields and green hedges, this is a distant view of the small village, strung out along a single lane and lying halfway between Wincanton and Sparkford. In the centre can just be discerned the Perpendicular west tower of St Michael's church. The building includes a Norman south doorway and font but has suffered the customary brutal Victorian restoration.

The estate here was granted to Glastonbury Abbey by King Edgar in the 10th century, to Turstin FitzRolf by 1086, to the bishop in 1275 and by enforced sale to the Duke of Somerset in 1548. More recently it was bought in 1826 by the Hunt family of nearby Compton Pauncefoot. The place gave a title to Lord Blackford (died 1947), a successful barrister who lived at Compton Castle.

BLAGDON The appropriately-named 'black hill' lies at the north-western end of the Mendips, the lofty Perpendicular tower (116 ft) of St Andrew's church high above the waters of Blagdon Lake reservoir (constructed 1899-1901). The body of the church, already rebuilt once in 1822, was rebuilt yet again in 1907-9 by Lord Winterstoke (died 1911) of the Wills tobacco company of Bristol. The noble lord took his title from Winterstoke Hundred in which Blagdon lies but he died childless in 1911, and his barony became extinct. The Wills family lived at Coombe Lodge at the head of the reservoir, rebuilt in imitation-Tudor style 1930-2. The Rev Augustus Toplady was curate here 1762-4 and, being caught in a storm in the nearby Burrington Combe, took shelter in a cleft there and was inspired to write the well-known hymn, 'Rock of Ages'.

BOSSINGTON Flower-decked cottages in this popular coastal hamlet north-east from Porlock, which is focused on a village green edged with willow and walnut trees. The manor here was held before the Norman Conquest by Athelney Abbey and, although granted to Ralph de Limesi by 1086, it later returned to the abbey to be sublet by the monks to Talbot of Heathfield and his Talbot family descendants. Later owners included the Sydenham family by 1472 until 1694, who presumably built the small chapel of about 1520 near their manor house at Lynch. The manor was bought from the Sydenhams by William Blackford of Holnicote, descending through the Dyke family to swell the considerable Acland estate on Exmoor.

BRADFORD-ON-TONE Trees frame the middle of this rewarding settlement which sits above the River Tone between Taunton and Wellington. Once the river must have been spanned by the 'broad ford' which christened it, but now traffic crosses a picturesque 15th century bridge at the foot of the hill. To the left of the picture is the village pub, the White Horse Inn, while beyond is the church of St Giles, flanked by mature trees and dating from about 1300 with a 15th century south chapel and early 16th century west tower. Here was held the funeral of Phyllis Perry, who died aged 94 in 1759 leaving a grand total of 201 children, grandchildren and great-grandchildren, most of whom attended the ceremony. There are wonderful views across the valley of the Tone to the Brendon and Quantock hills, marred only by the ubiquitous electricity pylons. Is it a fond hope that one day we will be able to afford to put such features where they belong – underground ?

BROMPTON REGIS The main village street under a cloudless sky, looking up the slope towards the church of St Mary the Virgin, with its 13th century west tower. Our second picture depicts a tranquil corner of its churchyard. A 17th century brass in the church commemorates members of the Dyke family, including 19-year-old Joan:

> *Shee dyed young; and soe oftimes 'tis seen,*
> *The fruit God loves, he's pleased to pluck it greene.*

The manor here, held by Gytha, mother of Harold, the last Saxon king, was seized by William the Conqueror – from which derives the suffix 'regis', meaning 'of the king'. By the later 12th century the estate had passed to William de Say who established Barlynch Priory, a small Augustininan monastery which he founded beside the River Exe in the west of the parish and of which some stonework survives in the fabric of Barlynch Farm. Say's successors in the 13th century, the Besils, founded a market and two fairs in the village and a castle at Bury. Nearby, the Wimbleball Lake Water Park is noted for its fishing and sailing and as a popular venue for picnics, as well as for supplying most of the water for Taunton, Tiverton and Exeter.

BROOMFIELD The highest village on the Quantocks, here seen under snow. As long ago as 1791 it was described as always 'remarkably healthy, even in times of general sickness elsewhere'. Owned in 1066 by Alnod, the manor was granted after the Conquest to William de Mohun, lord of Dunster, but was for centuries held with Crowcombe manor by the de Crowcombe family and their descendants, the Biccombes. The church of All Saints dates from the early 14th century and houses a fine set of Quantock benchends by the Bicknoller craftsman, Simon Warman.

Here since 1974 at Fyne Court, seen in our second picture, has been based Somerset Wildlife Trust (formerly the Somerset Trust for Nature Conversation). Fyne Court's mansion, destroyed by fire in 1894, was home to the Crosse family from the 17th century. Its members included the notorious Andrew Crosse (1784-1855), pioneer electrician, who was known locally as 'the Thunder and Lightning Man' and is thought by some to have been Mary Shelley's inspiration for her novel *Frankenstein*.

BURROWBRIDGE The chapel of St Michael on Burrow Mump silhouetted against the sky, below which the small village of Burrowbridge skirts the base of the hill. Until the recent (1994) discovery of 32 missing pages from the only known copy of Athelney Abbey's Cartulary (book of charters), the chapel here was first recorded only in 1480 by travelling topographer William of Worcester. The recovered pages, however, include a grant by Bishop Jocelin of the patronage of the chapel of St Michael of 'la Burgh', dated 1231-2, and thus pushes the chapel's history back a further 250 years. The same pages indicate that the Mump was known to the Saxons as *Reodbeorh* – 'reed hill'. The chapel, often described as ruined, is in fact unfinished, a proposed rebuilding in 1793 having failed to raise sufficient funds to complete the project. It was also the site of a Civil War skirmish in 1645 when royalist troops sought refuge there after the Battle of Langport.

BUTCOMBE The village climbs the side of 'Buda's valley', known beyond its bounds mainly for the quality of its Butcombe Ales, products of the local brewery. There was a mill here at the time of Domesday (1086), its site recalled only by the later Mill Inn. The small Perpendicular church of St Michael was over-restored in 1868 but retains its ornate south tower.

BUTLEIGH An incredibly English scene in high summer: reading from the left – cricket pavilion, church and Victorian pile. The church of St Leonard is mainly 14th century with the addition of transepts in 1851 and north aisle of 1859. Its monuments have made it a shrine to successive lords of the manors of both Butleigh and Butleigh Wootton. The former included James, Baron Glastonbury (died 1825), and Robert Grenville (died 1936), inventor of the Grenville Steam Carriage in 1875.

Butleigh Court was designed in 1845 by J.C. Buckler for the Dean of Windsor, George Neville Grenville. The other manor, centred on Wootton House, passed to the naval Hood (later Acland-Hood) family by marriage in 1792 and there they live still. Two sons of Butleigh rector, the Rev Samuel Hood, became admirals and were ennobled as Viscount Hood and Viscount Bridport, the former commemorated by a tall Tuscan pillar on nearby Windmill Hill.

CARHAMPTON The approach to this ancient village, sited in a sheltered dip on the main Taunton to Minehead road. As the meeting place of Carhampton Hundred, a Saxon administrative area which included Dunster, it was probably the oldest settlement in the area and a customary rent of 12 sheep was rendered to the manor by both Allerford and Oare.

The manor was retained by the West Saxon kings, being mentioned in King Alfred's will, until after 1066 when it was granted to William de Mohun of Dunster, being sold to the Luttrells in 1376. There is an Iron Age fort, known as Cæsar's Camp or Bat's Castle, on a nearby hill, traditionally linked with the 6th century Welsh St Carantoc and the Vikings

defeated the West Saxon king, Egbert, here in 836. The Perpendicular church of St John has a fine west tower, although rebuilt in 1870, and a 15th century rood screen repainted in its medieval colours.

CHARLTON HORETHORNE

A leafy prospect of this attractive village, sited at the junction of five roads near Wincanton. It was formerly known as Charlton Camville from its 12th and 13th century lords and is centred on a small village green overlooked by the 17th century manor house with its elaborate gate piers and the Kings Arms. Its later and present name identifies it as the meeting place of Horethorne Hundred.

For a second picture of the village see the glorious photograph on the front jacket of this book, with the flag of St George flying from the Perpendicular tower of the parish church of SS Peter and Paul. One farmer here, unpopular with his neighbours, does not lie in its churchyard. He left instructions that he should be buried in one of his own fields with a headstone to be inscribed:

Better to lie among thistles and briars
Than in a churchyard among thieves
and liars.

CHEDDAR The hexagonal Market Cross in the centre of this large village, indicating the sites of its former markets and fairs: the economic focus from the 13th century of the bishops' manor where the livestock and produce of the Mendips changed hands for generations. Even earlier the nearby Gorge with its caves was the home of man from the Old Stone Age, and in the grounds of a modern Comprehensive school the trowel of the archæologist has revealed a succession of noble timber halls of the West Saxon kings, dating from the 9th century. But to the wider world Cheddar means cheese, made here in the 17th century on a communal basis, by which all the milk from the area's cows was literally pooled on a daily basis and used to make one large cheese. Cheddar cheese is now produced here mainly for the tourist and the region is perhaps better known today for its market-gardening and the succulent strawberries that are its principal product.

CHEDZOY The rustic surroundings of the church of St Mary in the centre of this Levels village towards the western end of the Polden Hills. One of the simpler of Somerset's Perpendicular west towers was added to a building whose arcades date back to the 13th century. Initials in an elaborate panel of 1579 over the south porch are unlikely to be those of Abbot Richard Bere of Glastonbury, as often stated, since the church was held by Buckland Priory in Durston from the 12th century. From the same church tower the dispositions of the royalist forces before the Battle of Sedgemoor were observed by William Sparke, who sent news back to the Duke of Monmouth in Bridgwater. The rector of Chedzoy, Andrew Paschall, tried to dissuade his parishioners from joining the rebels, placed an eight-man guard on the village and then fled to Honiton with his family. On his return, Paschall compiled a detailed account of the campaign and a year later greeted James II at Bridgwater, having 'ye honour of being remembred by his Majesty and of kissing his hand'.

CHEW MAGNA A road junction in this sizeable village (or 'townelet' as Leland called it in the 16th century), which lies south-west from Keynsham. Taking its name from its situation on the River Chew, it is 'magna', 'the great', to distinguish it from the much smaller Chew Stoke. The principal manor was held by the bishops of Wells from Saxon times until its forced sale to the Duke of Somerset in 1548 although, apart from a gateway, the episcopal manor house to the east of the church has been almost entirely replaced by the Victorian Chew Court. The bishops established a borough here and the economy long depended on successful cloth manufacture: reflected in the high quality of its older houses and substantial 15th century church of St Andrew with a superb west tower. There are some Norman fragments in the church and a good rood screen, but the building is particularly notable for its superb memorials, including those to the St Loe, Baber and Strachey families of Sutton Court. At the entrance to the churchyard, recently restored, is the Church House of about 1500, evidently built by the St Loes, whose arms it bears. For its former role in maintaining the church fabric see Crowcombe.

CHEW STOKE Twin-arched picturesque bridge at the foot of Pilgrim's Way, which gives acress to the village street of attractive 18th century houses. Lying to the south-west of Chew Magna, the village's name means 'place belonging to Chew', possibly referring to its position within Chew Hundred. Above the village, the Perpendicular church of St Andrew was subjected to a brutal restoration in 1862. The fascinating Old Rectory, garnished with the arms of the St Loe lords of the manor and other families, is dated 1529 and was built by the then rector, John Barry. Later converted into the parish workhouse, it also attracted unfortunate Victorian attention. The Bilbie family had an important bell foundry here throughout the 18th and into the 19th centuries. The first bell at Keynsham bears the boastful inscription:

I value not who doth me see
For Thomas Bilby casted me,
Althow my sound it is but small
I can be heard amongst you all.

CHILTON CANTELO The bellcot of Chilton Cantelo House, overlooking the churchyard. The house, now used as a private school, was built by John Goodford, High Sheriff in 1816, shortly before his death in 1835. John's second son, Dr Charles Old Goodford (1812-84), managed to serve the rectory of Chilton while simultaneously headmaster and provost of Eton College. He was also responsible for rebuilding the church of St James in 1865 although he spared the Perpendicular west tower. The place is most widely known for the so-called 'screaming skull' of Theophilus Brome (died 1670). This is still kept in a small cupboard at Higher Farm, opposite the church, Brome having apparently requested this. Attempts to remove and bury the gruesome relic were said as long ago as 1791 to have been greeted with 'horrid noises, portentive of sad displeasure'.

CLAPTON-IN-GORDANO Set on the hillside of the Gordano valley, the appropriately-dedicated church of St Michael (right) and Clapton Court (centre) stand just below the dramatic sweep of the M 5 before it descends towards Bristol. The church is largely 13th century, although a Norman tympanum remains above the south doorway, and there is a north chapel of about 1300, which Pevsner considered was originally detached and Robert Dunning thought might have been the earlier one-cell church. The benchends at the west end of the nave have been assigned to the early 14th century, the oldest in Somerset, and the tower screen may be even older: moved from the manor house in the 19th century. The Court has a 15th century three-storey porch tower and old front wall, built by the Arthur lords of the manor and occupied by their descendants, the Wynters. Both Court and church are some half-a-mile from the small village, clustered around the old Black Horse, believed to be the former parish lock-up.

CLAVERTON The street of stone houses in this attractive village, 'settlement at the burdock ford', on the western side of the Avon valley and just south-east from Bath. Left by Saxon noblewoman Wulfwaru to her son Wulfmaer in about 1000, the manor passed to the bishops of Wells within half a century of the Norman Conquest and they held it until its enforced surrender in 1548. The bishops had a country retreat here east of the church, from which many of their letters and charters were issued, but even the succeeding manor house, supposed to have been damaged in the Civil War, has been swept away. The church of St Mary was over-restored from 1858 and its main interest lies in the churchyard: the substantial mausoleum of Ralph Allen (died 1764), postmaster and developer of Bath. Higher up the slope, designed by Sir Jeffry Wyatville 1819-20, is the later Claverton Manor, a fine villa which since 1961 has housed the American Museum.

COMBE HAY A magical prospect across the park to the south façade of the manor house with the church behind and the village beyond. Set in its deep valley, it was held until the 13th century by the Hawey family, a form of whose name was added to that of the manor, and then by their descendants, the Stradlings until 1644. The church (of unknown dedication) has a Perpendicular west tower but the rest was rebuilt in about 1760, according to Collinson, and the south aisle added by the then lord, Samuel Butler, in 1874. The house has a nine-bay west front of about 1730 and a slightly later south front, originally built by lawyer Robert Smith (died 1755), who inherited the manor from his father-in-law, Thomas Bennett.

COMBE ST NICHOLAS The village green at the heart of this valley settlement to the north-west of Chard. Granted to the Bishop of Wells after the Norman Conquest, in 1234 it was assigned to the provost of Wells Cathedral and to support no fewer than fifteen members of the Cathedral Chapter. When the office of provost was abolished, the estate passed to the deans of Wells. Evidence of Bronze-Age man was found at Combe Beacon in 1935 and the foundations of a Roman villa, complete with tessellated pavements, were unearthed at the hamlet of Wadeford in 1810. A small museum of finds is housed in the parish church of St Nicholas, a building largely reconstructed in the 15th century.

COMPTON BISHOP Below the smooth slope of the Mendip Hills nestles this charming village, probably given to the bishops of Wells by King Cnut (Canute). The manor was 'taken away' by King Harold who died at Hastings, but returned to the bishops by William the Conqueror and retained by them until 1548. At the righthand edge of the picture can be seen the Perpendicular west tower of the church of St Andrew, commanding extensive prospects over the Somerset Levels. The church was confirmed to Wells Cathedral by Pope Alexander III in 1176 and used to endow a Prebendal stall there. Richard the Lionheart licensed the bishop to establish a borough and port in the parish at Radclive (now Rackley) in 1189 but the investment proved an economic flop and there is little physical evidence of this medieval 'new town' today.

COMPTON DUNDON A valley view of Compton, one of the twin villages which with the hilltop settlement of Dundon make up Compton Dundon. Set in a green rolling landscape with wooded hills, midway between Street and Somerton, it is little surprise that the area attracted the Romans, who established villas at Littleton in the south of the parish. The manor was granted to Glastonbury Abbey by King Cynewulf of the West Saxons in 762, although the abbot had granted it away to Algar by 1066 and, after the Norman Conquest, it passed to Roger de Courcelles. A three-day fair around 22 July and a Thursday market were granted to the lady of the manor, Cecily de Beauchamp, in 1289 and this may have been linked with a planned borough laid out along Compton Street with a market cross, but this never materialised. In 1815 £3,000 was spent here digging for coal: fortunately in vain.

COMPTON MARTIN The houses climb the north Mendip slope, where the high pastures meet their back gardens. The manor, held by Serlo de Burci in 1086 was granted by the 12th century to the Martin family, whose name was added to that of the village to distinguish it from all the other places named Compton – 'valley settlement' – in Somerset. The mill pond in the village formerly powered a mill producing paper until about 1830. Today it is the source of the River Yeo, contributor to Blagdon Lake. Compton's treasure is the hillside church of St Michael which for Pevsner is the finest Norman church in the county. Despite a Perpendicular remodelling, much of the Norman work survives, including the finely carved chancel arch, both arcades, clerestory, chancel and font. A 13th century effigy in the north aisle has been identified with a member of the Moreton family which took its name from a Domesday manor to the north of the main village. Here was born St Wulfric, 12th century hermit and prophet, who found fame after he was immured at Haselbury Plucknett.

COMPTON PAUNCEFOOT The spire of the church of St Andrew, all but hidden in the centre of this delightful village, with its manicured lawns and hedges. The second part of the village's name is that of the Pauncefoot family, lords here from the 12th to the 16th centuries, the word being a Norman nickname meaning 'round belly'. It was Sir Walter Pauncefoot (died 1485) who contributed to the rebuilding of the church. The manor was acquired in about 1630 by John Hunt, whose descendant, John Hubert Hunt (died 1830) built the Gothic extravaganza of Compton Castle and also, in about 1820, the attractive terrace of workers' housing (second picture) known as Waterloo Crescent.

CONGRESBURY The priest's house, a remarkable survival of about 1470, built by the executors of Bishop Thomas Bekynton, which is linked to the 19th century vicarage (left). The place was named for St Congar, a 6th century saint who was apparently buried here after, according to legend, planting his staff (*à la* Joseph of Arimathea) which duly took root and was long known as 'St Congar's walking stick'. There was certainly a 9th century monastery here, when King Alfred granted it to Bishop Asser, although it is doubtful whether it survived the Norman Conquest. The manor was given to Bishop Jocelin by King John and the bishops obtained a market and fair here, their site presumably marked by a stepped cross. The church of St Andrew (*not* St Congar !) is outwardly Perpendicular but clearly a remodelling of its 13th century predecessor. Today Congresbury is a popular commuter village for Bristol with much modern building but retaining a gratifying number of old inns. The local pronunciation of its name ('Combesbury') is dying fast, thanks to the adverse influence of local TV and radio.

CORFE A terrace of whitewashed cottages lining the road which drops down from the Blackdown Hills towards Taunton. And it was towards Taunton that Corfe looked from Saxon times as a tithing within the bishop of Winchester's extensive manor of Taunton Deane. The church of St Nicholas, a neo-Norman rebuilding of 1842 on the east side of the road through the village, was formerly a chapelry of neighbouring Pitminster. To this was added a tower and aisle in 1858. The churchyard, where my parents-in-law are buried, has one of the most glorious outlooks to the wooded hills to the east. Taunton Priory had an estate which spanned the boundary with Pitminster, bought in 1543 by lawyer Humphrey Colles. Although Colles and his successors mainly chose to be buried at Pitminster they effectively became resident squires at Corfe. The 16th century mansion of Barton Grange, built by Colles, was largely demolished in 1931 and only the service wing survives, divided into flats.

CORTON DENHAM The church of St Andrew dominates this small village to the south-east of Sparkford. It looks medieval but was rebuilt 1869-70, having been designed by C. B. Green. The manor here was held by the Dinant (later Dynham) family by the 12th century and retained by them until 1509, a form of their surname being added to the Saxon name for the village: 'Corfetone' – 'settlement in a cutting'. More recent lords have included from about 1600 the Portmans of Orchard Portman, Viscount Portman having given a cemetery and mortuary chapel in 1910.

COSSINGTON A charming meeting of lanes in this attractive little village: one of a string which line the northern slopes of the Polden Hills. We shall never know anything more of Cusa, whose people named the place, but in common with many of these Polden settlements it passed to Glastonbury Abbey in Saxon times.

Later it was held for over four centuries from 1254 by the Brent family. In the village is the stump of an elm tree, improbably claimed to have received a fleeing Duke of Monmouth among its branches and, more likely, to have sheltered John Wesley on a preaching visit to the parish.

CROSCOMBE Two views on the main road between Wells and Shepton Mallet in this attractive village below the Mendip Hills. The larger building is known as the Old Manor House and includes a 15th century stone-vaulted ceiling with initials identified as those of Abbot John Selwood of Glastonbury (1456-93). The manor here was indeed given by King Ine to Glastonbury Abbey as early as 705 as part of Pilton, but had been granted away by 1086, so that an identification with John Selwood seems unlikely. Of later lords, the Paltons were responsible for much of the 15th century rebuilding of the fine parish church of the Virgin Mary, while it was the Fortescues who provided much of what is the finest interior woodcarving in the county, including a superb lofty screen and an ornate pulpit of 1616. The stepped village cross, saved from demolition in the 1870s by an early village 'sit-in', testifies to the site of a former market and fair granted in 1343.

CROWCOMBE The proximity of church, former rectory, church house and attractive war memorial forms a delightfully harmonious group – enhanced by the view up the drive in the lower photograph to the substantial Crowcombe Court. Built by MP Thomas Carew between 1724 and 1739, the Court was considered by Pevsner the finest Somerset house of its date south of Bath. The wooded Quantock hillside behind the building was also planted by Carew, although the parkland setting was the work of his son-in-law, James Bernard, who swept away the ornamental gardens around the house. The church house (centre) built in about 1515, is the finest survival of the many that used to feature in almost every Somerset village. They were used for fundraising by brewing and baking until the earlier 17th century to maintain the church. Although the place was a former borough with its own weekly market and annual fair from the 13th century, it has been a peaceful retreat since it was bypassed by the present Taunton to Minehead road in 1929.

CUCKLINGTON The church of St Lawrence dates from the 13th century but was much restored 1873-80. Its attractive little bellcot was added to accommodate the bell for the tower clock: probably in 1705 after the church had been damaged in a notorious storm two years earlier. The building stands picturesquely at the end of a narrow lane and commands wonderful outlooks westwards towards Wincanton. Surprisingly an attempt was made to commercialise this little village in 1304 when its lord, Henry de Lorty, obtained a grant of a shortlived market and fair. The manor was held with that of nearby Stoke Trister, later passing with it to the powerful Phelips family of Montacute House, several of whom were rectors here in the 18th and 19th centuries.

CURRY RIVEL The daisy-packed village green flanked by thatched cottages, its northern limit closed by the Perpendicular church of St Andrew: a view missed by those travelling through on the main road from Taunton to Langport. 'Curry' is a British stream name to which has been added the surname of Richard Revel who obtained the manor in 1190. The church is full of fascinating memorials to former lords and other wealthy parishioners of the past, including a fine series of four 13th century effigies to members of the Lorty family, descendants of the Revels, in the north chapel. Another tomb bears the cavalier figures of Marmaduke Jennings (died 1625) and his son of nearby Burton Pynsent, an estate which was left in 1765 to Prime Minister, William Pitt the elder, later Earl of Chatham. The church includes the hatchment of Pitt's widow and a memorial to one of her servants.

DINDER Looking east along the main street of the village, charmingly fronting the River Sheppey. The manor was one of the earliest endowments of the bishopric of Wells but was granted away by the 12th century. The Somervilles inherited the estate from the Hickes family in the 18th century and the Rev George William Somerville built Dinder House, a large Georgian mansion of 1801-3, at the western edge of the village beside the Perpendicular church of St Michael. The latter was a chapelry of Wells and from 1268 endowed a prebend in Wells Cathedral. A Norman carving of a dragon's head in the chancel survives from an earlier church, there is an elaborate carved pulpit of 1621 and a profusion of Somerville memorials.

DOWLISH WAKE A corner of the road in the centre of this secluded village south-east from Ilminster: on the skyline the tower of St Andrew's church and to the right the Dower House, dated 1674 and occupied by ladies of the Speke family in the later 18th century. The Spekes inherited the manor in 1420 and hold the lordship still, their title traced back through the Kaynes family to the Wakes, lords by the later 12th century. The church, served by an illiterate rector in 1322, had opposition between about 1811 and 1849 from Edmund Baker, who,

having won over Jane Parke and her sister, based himself at Parke House and converted 100 local people to the eccentric sect of Joanna Southcott, a Devonshire prophetess.

The second picture depicts Perry's Cider Mill which now regularly brings tourists to the village to sample and purchase the county's traditional beverage. Indeed, the 1851 Census revealed that one third of the total population here (322) were surnamed Perry!

DUNSTER A lofty prospect from the castle hill down towards the High Street under bunting and the octagonal Yarn Market of about 1590. Strictly speaking Dunster is not a village but a former successful clothmaking and trading town: largely preserved because of its abrupt decline in the 18th century and the paternal care of its lords. After the Norman Conquest the place was granted to William de Mohun who built his castle in a commanding position on 'Dunn's tor' and his descendants had established a borough here by 1197 with a market in High Street by 1222. The Luttrells bought both castle and manor from the Mohuns in 1375, and from 1404 made it their home, ruling a West Somerset empire which included the neighbouring town of Minehead. There was a priory here, whose ornate church survives as the parish church of St George, with some remnants of the priory buildings to the north. The castle, probably the most romantically situated anywhere in England and held by the National Trust since 1976, has been rebuilt and remodelled several times but remains a fascinating treasure house of furniture and paintings, with delightful hillside gardens.

EAST COKER Daffodils decorate this lovely Hamstone village to the south-west of Yeovil, where thatched cottages proliferate and an air of peace pervades its lanes. It was this peace which enchanted the American poet, T.S. Eliot, who traced his ancestry to a 17th century emigrant from here, Andrew Eliot, and in 1965 requested burial of his own ashes in the church of St Michael. The same building includes memorials to another native, buccaneer and explorer William Dampier (1651-1715), as well as those to successive lords of the manor who lived in happy seclusion at Coker Court beside the church. One of their number, Archdeacon William Helyar, founded the attractive 17th century almshouses which line the path down from both church and court, and are seen here in our second picture.

EAST LYNG The view from the church tower towards Athelney and beyond shows how the village lines a ridge above the Somerset Levels, flooded here in this winter photograph. Formerly almost isolated by inland water and marshes, it was fortified by the West Saxon kings against Viking attack and linked by bridge to a neighbouring fort at Athelney. The place was long ruled by the monks of Athelney Abbey, founded immediately east of the village by King Alfred in thanksgiving for his victory over the Danish king, Guthrum, at the battle of Edington (Wilts). The cultivation of withies (willows) and making of baskets dates here from the late 18th century.

EAST QUANTOXHEAD The former mill pond, whose head of water probably drove the mill recorded here in 1086 until grinding ceased in the 1920s. The mill building which survives today was rebuilt in 1729 following a fire which destroyed its predecessor. After the Norman Conquest the delightful small village was granted to Ralph Pagnell and over nine centuries later is still held by his descendant, Sir Walter Fownes Luttrell, who occupies the Court House: a record of continuous ownership unique for Somerset. Its outbuildings can be seen in our picture beside the small church of St Mary: dating from the early 14th century and fortunately spared the hand of the Victorian restorer. Here was born without arms or legs Sarah Biffin (1784-1850), a celebrated mouth painter, 'discovered' by the Earl of Morton and patronized by royalty.

ENMORE Today the centre of this village on the eastern slopes of the Quantocks, ruled by the Malet family throughout the Middle Ages, gives little hint of the 18th century make-over it suffered at the hands of the 2nd Earl of Egmont, builder in the 1750s of the incredible dry-moated Enmore Castle.

The money troubles of the 4th Earl led to the sale of his estate to Nicholas Broadmead from Milverton, who demolished all but a fragment of the Castle and whose family in turn dominated the parish until 1954. The Rev John Poole, founded a model school in the village in 1810 and five years later

published *The Village School Improved.* Of his predecessors as rector, one was described as 'worn out' in 1327, another as 'distracted of his wits' in 1554 and a 17th century cleric earned complaints because his sermons continued until 5 in the afternoon.

FARLEIGH HUNGERFORD The ruins of Farleigh Castle, founded in about 1383 by Sir Thomas Hungerford, Speaker of the House of Commons, and with a bloody history unequalled in the county, are not an obvious candidate for a book on Somerset villages. In the centre of the picture, however, is the mid 14th century castle chapel which was the original parish church of St Leonard. As such it was presumably the focus of the Saxon village of Farleigh, given by King Ethelred to his huntsman Leofwine in 987. When Walter, Lord Hungerford, extended the castle from about 1420, he evidently swept away the existing village and built a new Perpendicular parish church, consecrated in 1443, to the south of the castle together with dwellings for his tenants. The only member of the royal family known to have been born in Somerset first saw the light of day at Farleigh in 1473: Margaret daughter of George, Duke of Clarence (he of the butt of Malmesey), and niece of Richard III.

FRESHFORD The fine stone-built village, south-east from Bath, with (centre) the former brewery and its slender chimney. The place takes its name from a 'freshwater ford' presumably marked by the bridge over the River Frome, rebuilt in 1783. The manor was held by the monks of Hinton Charterhouse from their priory's foundation in 1232 until its dissolution in 1540, but bought in the early 18th century by the Methuens of Corsham, Wiltshire. The principal industry here was cloth manufacture, at its height in the 18th and 19th centuries and based chiefly at Dunkirk and Freshford mills. The church of St Peter stands on the hill above the village with a short 15th century tower, the rest rebuilt in the 19th century.

GREINTON Looking out over the village across the Levels from the lower slope of the Polden Hills. The farms and cottages are built of the local blue lias stone and are strung out along the meandering Taunton to Glastonbury road. Indeed, it was Glastonbury Abbey which owned the estate here before the Norman Conquest, as it held so many manors in the vicinity of the Poldens. To the right of the picture is the church tower of St Michael and All Angels, garnished with gargoyles: a building heavily restored by the Victorians but containing a good series of benchends dated 1621. In the later 17th century the place became a refuge from Anglican persecution for local Quakers. These included the Clark family who in 1750 moved down the road to Street, where from 1825 they laid the foundations of what became the greatest shoemaking company in Europe.

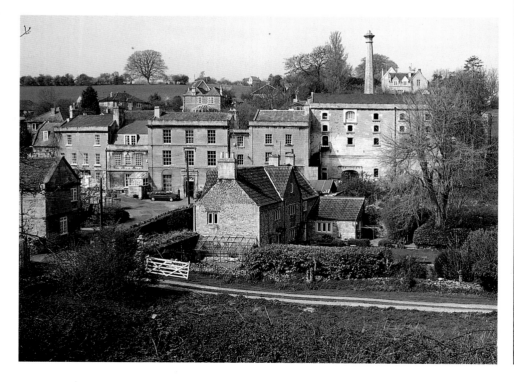

HIGH HAM The picture shows the village green with the church of St Andrew: its churchyard described in 1598 as 'compassed aboute with tall and goodly elmes'. Many of the village houses enjoy splendid views over the Somerset Levels and the location attracted the Romans, who built two villas in the parish. The manor was granted in the 10th century to Glastonbury Abbey by King Edgar, and Abbot John Selwood was chiefly responsible for rebuilding the church nave of 1476-77 onto the early 14th century west tower. Of the 16th century priests who ministered here, John Helpes, a former Glastonbury monk, died from gorging himself on brawn, and John Kenell, parson 1560-70, 'meanly lerned and very olde', who spent £400 on 'a most notorious harlot', married 'a rustique, rude and foolish woman' and died in poverty at London, aged over 90.

HINTON BLEWETT The charming focus of this small village, west from Midsomer Norton, looking from the bollarded village green, known as the Barbury, to a terrace of cottages, beyond which peeps the west tower (rebuilt in the 18th century) of the Perpendicular All Saints church. There is a Norman font and a pulpit with tester dated 1638. The Bluets who named the place were lords of the manor during the 14th and 15th centuries.

HINTON CHARTERHOUSE A small village beside the road south from Bath. Here Ela, Countess of Salisbury, founded in about 1232 a priory of Carthusian monks (whence 'Charterhouse') at the same time that she established Laycock Abbey, Wiltshire. In the late 15th century one of the monks, Stephen of Flanders, was notorious for his visions of St Mary Magdalene. Another brother, Nicholas Hopkins, mentioned twice by Shakespeare, was an intimate of the unfortunate Duke of Buckingham and prophesied that Buckingham, beheaded in 1521, would succeed Henry VIII on the throne. In consequence he spent some time in the Tower and probably died there. There was also resistance to the dissolution in 1540 from the prior and several of the brethren. To the right of the picture are the substantial priory remains, including the chapter house, sacristy and the undercroft of the refectory, although nothing remains of the priory church.

HINTON ST GEORGE

A wonderfully unspoilt Hamstone village to the north-west of Crewkerne, preserved because it lay away from the main roads and was governed by its lords in almost feudal fashion until recent times. The manor was held by the Denebaud family from the 13th century until 1429, their heiress carrying it to her husband, William Poulett, great-grandfather of Sir Amias Poulett, gaoler of Mary, Queen of Scots. The Pouletts secured a barony in 1627 and an earldom in 1706, continuing until the death of the 8th Earl without issue in 1973. Their former grand mansion, Hinton House, is now subdivided into separate apartments. The church of St George, whose dedication provides the village with its suffix, has a west tower which was probably being built in 1487 when the rector of Horsington bequeathed £2 towards the cost. It contains a magnificent 'valhalla' of memorials to the Pouletts, who even had their coat of arms added to the 13th century font.

HORSINGTON A quiet flower-fringed street east of the main road north to Castle Cary. This 'horsekeeper's settlement' (compare with the name of nearby Henstridge: 'the ridge where stallions were kept') was held by Savard and Eldeva in 1066 but granted to William son of Wido after the Norman Conquest. The village features a substantial 18th century manor house, the early 19th century mansion of the Dodington family (now Horsington Hotel) and a high stepped village cross. The Wickhams were rectors here continuously for over two centuries from 1686, living at the 18th century rectory, now the Grange, and twice virtually rebuilt the parish church of St John the Baptist: in 1819 and 1885-7.

HUTTON A rustic panorama of this small village with the church of St Mary (right) and the tower of the former manor house, Hutton Court (left). It is hard to believe that this secluded spot lies only 4 miles east of the centre of Weston-super-Mare. The name of the place means 'settlement (under?) the spur of the hill', presumably referring to the wooded ridge which shelters it. The present Court, including a fine dining hall, dates from the late 15th century and was probably begun by John Payne (died 1496), commemorated on a brass in the church, as is his son Thomas (died 1528). The Paynes sold out in 1604 to Bishop John Still, to whom is attributed the Jacobean range behind the Court. The Court's west front of about 1700 was probably added by the Codrington descendants of Bishop Still. In his record of the marriage of William Pimm here in 1793 the minister noted that 'when I came to that part of the ceremony on the woman's part "Obey him," etc, Pimm bawled out "Stop, sir, please to read that over again. The women don't rightly understand it".'

ISLE ABBOTTS Church tower and cottages in this small village to the north of Ilminster. The village on the River Isle was held from Saxon times until 1538 by Muchelney Abbey, from which derives the suffix 'abbotts'. Original settlement was probably in the vicinity of the church, to the west of which a planned medieval settlement of three parallel lanes seems to have been added. The superb church of St Peter was built by the monks: its finely-detailed 15th century tower surprisingly retaining its statues in their niches. The chancel is earlier, dating from about 1300 and containing an excellent sedilia and piscina, and there is also an inverted Norman font bearing a dragon.

KELSTON Sunshine on old stone in this engaging little village, 'settlement where calves were reared', north-west from Bath on the road to Bristol and formerly known for its 18th century brass mill. The place is dominated by Kelston Park, a large plain house perched high above the wooded valley of the River Avon, designed in about 1770 by John Wood the Younger for the king's surgeon, Sir Cæsar Hawkins. Its predecessor was built near the church, probably in 1587, for the family of Sir John Harington (1561-1612), Elizabethan courtier, godson to the queen and hailed as the inventor of the water closet. He publicised his invention with a monograph entitled *A New Discourse of a Stale Subject called the Metamorphosis of Ajax*. Sadly his brilliant concept had to wait centuries for the advent of piped water before it was widely adopted. Before the Reformation the place was held by the abbesses of Shaftesbury, thereafter being granted to Audrey, illegitimate daughter of Henry VIII by Joan Dingley *alias* Dobson, who brought it (and Batheaston and St Catherine) in marriage to the Haringtons. The church of St Nicholas was largely rebuilt in 1860 but includes a piece of a 9th century carved cross.

KILMERSDON Down the hill towards the middle of this village, which lies towards the south-east of the Mendip Hills. The church of SS Peter and Paul may have been a Saxon minster and was long held by Buckland Priory in Durston. Although there are some Norman features: windows, a south doorway and an external frieze, these seem to have been reset in a 15th century rebuilding which included a high four-stage west tower. Set against the skyline is the column, apeing the former Eddystone Lighthouse, which was erected 1852-3 in memory of Thomas Samuel Jolliffe (died 1824), who built Ammerdown House in the parish 1789-91. His wife brought him half the manor and he later purchased the other. His descendants became baronets in 1821 and lords Hylton from 1866, taking their title from the home of their ancestors, the Hyltons of Hylton Castle in Sunderland.

Our second picture depicts 19th century workers' cottages in the village.

KINGSTON ST MARY Looking north from the fields which surround this attractive Quantock village to the hills which rise behind it. Its name suggests that it was once held by the kings of the West Saxons before it passed to the Saxon bishops of Winchester to form part of their extensive manor of Taunton Deane. Above the trees appears the superb late 15th century tower of St Mary's church, whose dedication completes the place's name and which was held by Taunton Priory and thereafter by the Dean and Chapter of Bristol Cathedral. The building includes a fine series of Quantock benchends, dated 1522, and a host of monuments to the former owners of Tetton, Tainfield and Hestercombe houses, the last once forming a detached part of the parish. The only drawback to the village's location is the fact that it lines the principal (and winding) road from Taunton up to the hills.

KINGSTON SEYMOUR The spired church of All Saints in this appealing low-lying village to the north-west of Yatton. Indeed, its situation on the Levels beside the Yeo led in 1607 to a fearsome 10-day flood in which many drowned, with five feet of water in the church. The manor, presumably once held by the West Saxon kings, was granted in the late 12th century to Milo de St Maur (Seymour), whence the latter part of the place's name. The west tower of the church is probably 14th century but the chancel was rebuilt in 1865.

KINGWESTON The church, manor house and park dominate this idyllic scene, but there is little here that is any earlier than the rebuilding of Kingweston House in the 1780s. What remains of the village lines the lane south-west from the house but most early settlement was probably swept away when the park was created. Agents for change were the Dickinson family, formerly Quakers from Bristol who amassed a fortune from sugar and slaves in the West Indies. In 1855 they also rebuilt the church of All Saints, designed with its slender spire by C. E. Giles, but retained the Norman font from the previous building. Kingweston House has been occupied by Millfield School since 1946.

LONG SUTTON. The Saxon centre of this 'southern settlement' (south from Somerton), focused on a picturesque village green. Earthworks to the south and east of the church testify to former houses and farms abandoned as people settled further to the north-east and north along the road, to give the place its adjective 'long' by the 14th century. This development was largely at the hands of the monks of Athelney Abbey, to whom King Alfred had given the main manor in the 9th century. The monks were also partly responsible for rebuilding Holy Trinity parish church, finished in 1493, although the church was given in about 1200 to endow a prebend in Wells Cathedral. Among those who ministered here was William Underhill, who took himself off in 1397 to improve his education, and John Towkere, removed in 1436 for subletting the church land and deserting his parish. A touching epitaph of about 1680 runs:

Sixteen years I was a maid,
Six months I was a wife,
One day I was a mother,
And so I end my life.

LUCCOMBE Views of this enchanting village close up and, from a distance, in its Exmoor setting. It lies isolated in 'Lufa's valley' (the meaning of its name) to the south-east of Porlock and was formerly held in two estates, the manors of East and West Luccombe: the latter centred on a second charming settlement at Horner, the former inherited by Sir Thomas Dyke Acland in 1802 under the will of the Earl of Strafford. As such the place became part of the Holnicote estate and is now held by the National Trust. Luccombe's peaceful ambience makes it an unlikely starting point for the troubles of Dr Henry Byam, rector here from 1615 and when the Civil War began. Turned out of the parsonage, he was imprisoned but escaped, joining the future Charles II in exile and following him to the Scilly Isles, Jersey and France. Of his five sons who served in the royalist army, two were killed and, in an attempt to join him, his wife and daughter were both drowned in the Bristol Channel. Byam returned to Luccombe rectory at the Restoration and died here in 1669 aged 89.

LULLINGTON Looking towards the church across the village green. Like Selworthy and West Quantoxhead, this picturesque village to the north of Frome is largely a 19th century creation by George Devey for William Duckworth, who bought it with the neighbouring estate of Orchardleigh in 1855. Duckworth ordered new thatched cottages, rectory, school and farms but he could only restore the church of All Saints. It is the finest small Norman church in the county, put up within 30 years of the Conquest with its superbly-detailed doorways, arches and font. The Duckworth monuments in the south chapel, including that of 1986 to Arthur Duckworth, the last of their short-lived four-generation Somerset dynasty, seem somewhat of an intrusion on an 11th century symphony.

LUXBOROUGH Brendon cottages in the hamlet of Kingsbridge, including the Royal Oak Inn. Nearby stands Chargot House, built in 1826 as a rural retreat and hunting box by Sir Thomas Buckler Lethbridge of Sandhill Park (Bishops Lydeard), who from 1839 began to mine for iron in the vicinity. From 1926 it was the secluded home of the Malet baronets. The parish church of St Mary, one of the most isolated possessions of Bruton Abbey, stands in the older hamlet of Churchtown and its chancel dates from the 13th century, its tower (with a later sadddleback roof) from the 14th. The remainder is largely Perpendicular although a north aisle was added and the nave mostly rebuilt in 1861. The parish encompassed a number of early manors which went under the colourful names of Luxborough Picot, Luxborough Everard, Luxborough Eve and Langham Tort.

LYMPSHAM Part of the 19th century face of this Victorian village created to the south of Weston-super-Mare by the Stephenson family. They made a more radical impression on the place in the hundred years that they were here than had Glastonbury Abbey during the eight centuries that the abbots held the manor. The Rev Joseph Adam Stephenson became rector in 1809 and built the pinnacled Manor House in about 1820, while his son, Preb Joseph Henry, criticised in 1847 for his over-long sermons, put up 17 houses here and built the picturesque Manor Hall in 1875. The 15th century church of St Christopher was completely transformed in order to glorify the Stephensons. They defaced the building with black-letter texts (even the medieval font), crammed the church with their memorials, and in 1863 even depicted the entire family in the stained glass of the east window.

MARSTON MAGNA Cottages and the former school (left) of 1841 opposite the church in the middle of this village, which lies to the north-east of Yeovil on the Hornsey brook. From its nine Saxon owners it passed after the Conquest to Robert, Count of Mortain, and later to the lords Beauchamp of Hatch Beauchamp. The fine church of St Mary the Virgin, with Norman font and chancel, was possessed by the Devonian nuns of Polsloe Priory until the dissolution of their house. In 1736, most unusually, the rectorial estate was granted to the vicars (who thus technically became 'rectors') by the trustees of Sir John St Barbe, formerly lord of the manor. The neighbouring Rectory was occupied by King Lewanika of Barotseland and his entourage while in England to attend the coronation of Edward VII.

MARTOCK The middle of this extensive central Somerset village is focused on the mid 18th century market house and adjoining pinnacle or market cross. The White Hart (right) occurs from 1736, was regularly used for public meetings and in 1864 Wildman's Theatre and even the Lyric Opera Company performed in its assembly rooms. A market was held here from 1247 until the 19th century, with an added fair on St Lawrence's day (10 August) by 1302. Clothmaking occurred from the 16th century, probably reaching its height in the 18th century at the hands of successful families such as the Coles, Pattens, Butlers, Hamlyns and Palmers. Its decline led to the development of gloving and, from the mid 19th century, canvas and heavy engineering.

The attractive two-storey Hamstone building in our second picture, since 1975 a private house opposite the church, was used as Martock's church house, court house and grammar school. The school was endowed in 1662 by William Strode of Barrington, the headmaster living on the ground floor, with the schoolroom on the first floor. Above the front door is still carved the name of God in Hebrew, Greek and Latin, the three languages once taught at the school, which closed in 1862. Daniel Defoe was entertained by the broad Somerset accent of some of the pupils when he visited in about 1720 and claimed kinship with the master.

MEARE The church of St Mary and Manor House Farm. The church was rededicated, presumably after a rebuilding, in 1323 and the tower and chancel evidently survive from that time. The manor house was built in about 1340 on an even older site by Abbot Adam de Sodbury of Glastonbury, the abbey having held the manor from the 7th century.

Long before this, from the 3rd century BC, there was an Iron-Age Lake village here, probably a seasonal summer market or fair. Later Meare provided a refuge for Beonna, a holy man, mistakenly identified as St Benignus, whose relics were translated to Glastonbury in 1091 and kept in a reliquary given by King Harthacnut. The saint was credited in legend with creating Meare Pool (originally called Ferramere) to provide himself and his followers with fish. Another story has Benignus planting his staff in the ground here so that it took root and flowered: a tale which later attached itself to St Joseph of Arimathea at Glastonbury.

MELLS One of the most beautiful villages in the county, its layout is the result of careful planning by its lords, the abbots of Glastonbury, to whom it was given by Earl Athelstan in the 10th century. New Street was one arm, the only one completed, of a cross-shaped development planned by Abbot John Selwood in about 1470. The church of St Andrew's ornate 104 ft west tower was being built in 1446 and the rest of the richly decorated building is also mainly 15th century. After the abbey's dissolution the manor was sold in 1543 to Thomas and John Horner, although there is no foundation for any link with the nursery rhyme of Little Jack Horner, as often claimed, since the character occurs from as far back as the 14th century. The Horners lived here until earlier this century and their descendants, the Asquiths, live here still in the elegant manor house to the west of the church.

MILVERTON Two views of peaceful terraced houses in North and High streets – more peaceful since 1975 when a new bypass opened to link Taunton and Wiveliscombe. While most visitors would consider it a village, the place was in fact a royal borough by 1265 and possibly even under the Saxons. It certainly had a market by 1086, a fair by 1280 and was long administered by a portreeve. There was a flourishing cloth manufacture until its 18th century decline and a silk-throwing factory from 1809. As well as a borough, it was the meeting place of Milverton Hundred and from 1226 the archdeacons of Taunton had a residence here: represented by the late 15th century building to the east of the substantial Perpendicular church of St Michael. Milverton's most famous son was Thomas Young, born in 1773 next to the Quaker meeting-house in North Street. He helped to decipher Egyptian hieroglyphics, formulated the wave theory of light and pioneered the study of optics.

MONTACUTE Strictly speaking this Hamstone haven is a town rather than a village, having become a borough at the hands of the counts of Mortain soon after the time of Domesday (1086). Indeed, the centre of the village, its former market place, is still known as the Borough and it is from that vantage point that our first picture was taken, looking up Middle Street towards St Michael's Hill. This hill was the *mons acutus* or 'sharp hill' which gave Montacute its present name, and the castle which once topped it was subjected to a Saxon attack in 1068.

To the north of the Borough Sir Edward Phelips, Speker of the House of Commons, built Montacute House in the 1590s, although Sir Edward did not acquire the manor itself until 1607-8. Our view is of the west front, added to the earlier house from the demolished Clifton Maybank House in Dorset. The result is the finest house in Somerset, its Long Gallery now crammed with fascinating paintings of Tudor and Stuart worthies from the National Portrait Gallery.

MUCHELNEY The remarkably-preserved thatched Priest's House (right) of 1308 stands opposite the parish church in this tiny village. It was described as 'ruinous' in 1606 and it seems unlikely that vicars lived there by the 18th century and it was spurned even by assistant curates by 1815. Later it was used as a cellar or school and only saved by its acquisition for the National Trust in 1911. (See also page 1 and the frontispiece picture on pages 2 and 3).

NEMPNETT THRUBWELL The church of St Mary stands on an elevated site at some distance from the scattered village, between Chew Valley and Blagdon lakes, and may represent the original area of settlement. The chancel was rebuilt in 1897, divided from the nave by an elaborate 19th century screen attributed to Pugin, but the Norman south doorway survives. The name of this place (with Haselbury Plucknett, one of the best loved in the county), recorded as 'Emnet' in about 1200, reflects its high situation and means 'the plain'. To this was added 'Thrubwell', a manor which formerly straddled the boundary with Butcombe to the west and was named from a 'gushing spring' there. A chambered barrow here called Fairy Toot was almost completely destroyed by rudimentary 18th century excavation, during which a pile of seven human skulls were found. In 1791 it was stated that 'strange noises have been heard underneath the hill and visions, portentious to children, have been seen waving in the thickets which crown its summit'.

NETHER STOWEY. Young riders heading up Castle Street, so named because it leads to the earthworks of a Norman castle built to the west of the village in the 12th century. Also in Castle Street lived Thomas Poole, a wealthy tanner, who attracted to his table a literary circle which included Robert Southey, Charles Lamb, Sir Humphrey Davy and, most significantly, William and Dorothy Wordsworth and Samuel Taylor Coleridge. Poole arranged for Coleridge to rent a cottage in Lime Street, 1797-99, while the Wordsworths stayed in more palatial lodgings at nearby Alfoxton in Holford. The place was a borough by 1225 with a market and fair from 1304, and cloth was produced here until the 18th century. Stowey Court was begun by James, Lord Audley (executed 1497), to the east of the village, although the present house is probably 16th century. Beside it stands the church of St Mary, a rebuilding of 1849-51, and both church and Court are severed from the rest of the village by the new course of the A39, developed in 1968.

NORTH CADBURY Looking across its lawns to North Cadbury Court and the tower of St Michael's church. The substantial manor house was largely rebuilt by Puritan MP, Sir Francis Hastings, after he received the estate from his brother, the Earl of Huntingdon, in 1586. Following the death of his first wife in 1596 he sold up and moved to Dorset, the house later being owned by the Newman (1684-1790) and Bennett (1790-1899) families. The village was the meeting place of Catash Hundred, whose name is preserved in Catash Inn, built in 1796.

The second picture shows the beech-lined lane running north to the village from both Court and church. At the rectory here until 1861 was kept by the Rev Richard Foley the 'box' of Joanna Southcott (1750-1814), the fanatical prophetess, and supposed to hold her final prophecies. When eventually opened it was found to contain a woman's nightcap and a lottery ticket !

NORTH CHERITON The church of St John the Baptist with adjacent stocks. The name 'Cheriton' ('church settlement'), recorded in 1086, suggests that this was a Saxon foundation. The present building has a Perpendicular west tower, but the rest largely dates from restorations and enlargements of 1878 and 1886. There is a Norman tub font, Jacobean pulpit and a rood screen constructed from fragments of carved timber (1498-1508) brought from Pilton church in 1883. More unusual items which are displayed on the walls of the church comprise the redundant clappers of four bells and the handcuffs once employed by the village constable.

NORTH CURRY The harvested fields extend close to the middle of the village, as shown in our first picture, and illustrate the prominent site of the church of SS Peter and Paul, with its central octagonal crossing tower of about 1300, although a Norman north door has been saved from an earlier building. A tablet in the vestry records the custom of the Reeve's Christmas feast, celebrated at least since 1192, at which a massive mince pie bearing the image of King John, grantor of a market and fair here in 1206, was consumed and the tenants swilled free ale as long as two one-pound candles continued to burn.

The second picture depicts Queen Square, likely site of both market and fair, with its 'pepper-pot' memorial to Queen Victoria. The manor here was probably an early possession of the West Saxon kings, passing to the bishop of Wells in 1189 and later to the dean and chapter.

NORTH NEWTON Narrow boats on the Bridgwater to Taunton Canal, built in 1827 and whose restoration was completed in 1994, pass close to this small village which until 1880 formed part of North Petherton parish. Although there has been much modern building, the place has a wealth of 17th century farmhouses and cottages and the 17th century church of St Peter. This began as the 13th century chantry chapel of the manor of Newton Placey and was furnished with an excellent carved screen, pulpit (dated 1637) and vestry door by Sir Thomas Wroth of nearby Petherton Park, but the fabric mainly dates from a rebuilding of 1884.

NORTON ST PHILIP The parish church of St Philip and (right) the castellated village school of 1827. The church was largely rebuilt in individual style by wealthy local clothier, Jeffrey Flower (died 1644), who entertained the queen of James I at his home, the Grange, now Manor Farm, in 1615. The area of the church probably represents the original village, the monks of nearby Hinton Charterhouse establishing a borough on the hill, which became a prominent clothmaking centre, with its own market and fair.

Also on the hill stands Norton's best known building, the 15th century George Inn, complete with a loft 'where the lynnen cloth is sould at the fare tymes'. The village was the scene of a bloody skirmish during the Monmouth Rebellion of 1685 in which some 100 men died, mainly royalists, but which persuaded the Duke to return south to eventual defeat at Sedgemoor. A further 12 rebels were hanged, drawn and quartered here after the Bloody Assizes: a brutal revenge long remembered in the area.

NUNNEY The north-west wall of Nunney Castle, placed on an ill-defended site within an oblong moat in the centre of the village of Nunney. Built by Sir John de la Mare, presumably soon after he had licence to crenellate his house here in 1373, it comprised a high-walled rectangle with drum towers at each corner. In design it has been compared to the French Bastille, a sketch of 1644 showing it with a high pitched roof and conical tops to the towers. It continued in the Delamare family and their descendants, the Paulets, until sold in 1577 to Richard Prater, member of a prominent Roman Catholic family. Prater's royalist grandson held the castle during the Civil War, until it surrendered to the Roundheads in 1645 after cannon fire breached its north-west wall: the only occasion on which it saw action during the six centuries since it was built. The castle was slighted by Parliament by having its roof and internal floors removed, although the wall only collapsed as recently as 1910.

Our second picture depicts the tower (of about 1500) of All Saints parish church, a building which contains memorials to many of the owners of the castle and the other former estates here.

OLD CLEEVE Roses around thatched cottage doors in this attractive West Somerset village. It is 'old' in contrast to Cleeve Abbey which lies further inland and was founded in the 'valley of flowers' by William de Roumare, Earl of Lincoln, in the late 12th century. The manor inevitably formed part of the abbey's endowment and a short-lived market and two fairs were established here in 1466. The church of St Andrew, dating from the 13th century, dominates the village, its west tower built in 1533 when John Tucker bequeathed his tucker's shears towards the completion of the work. An unidentified 15th century effigy has its feet resting on a cat with a mouse between its paws. One unfortunate curate here, John Trat, was murdered by four of his parishioners in 1614. They cut up his body and boiled and salted the pieces to stop them from smelling: a vain exercise as all four were hanged at Stone Gallows near Taunton.

OVER STOWEY The church and churchyard of SS Peter and Paul occupying an L-shaped corner in this picturesque Quantock village. The church's Perpendicular west tower and the nearby parsonage were fortified during the Civil War by royalist John Sellick. He rang the church bells to summon villagers to resist a Roundhead attack from Taunton 'in which many soldiers and commanders were slain'. The church itself was heavily restored by architect Richard Carver in 1840 but retains a good series of 16th century benchends and several attractive memorials, including those to the one and only Baron Taunton, Henry Labouchere (died 1869) and his descendants the Stanleys. Lord Taunton, long the MP for the county town of Taunton, bought up much of the parish and from 1857 built a substantial Victorian pile, Quantock Lodge, occupied by a private school since 1963.

PENDOMER A lane leaving this secluded village which lies to the east of Crewkerne on the county boundary with Dorset. Indeed, the place is sited at the end of a *cul-de-sac,* which presumably accounts for its unspoilt character. The second part of its name recalls the ownership of the manor by the Domer family (named for Dummer in Hampshire) from the 12th century until 1407. Among them was Sir John de Domer, returned as MP for Somerset in 1306 and 1313, who lies in effigy under an embattled cornice carried by two peasants in the Perpendicular parish church. The Domers presumably occupied the former manor house (rebuilt since their time) to the west of the church and in their day must have enjoyed the still splendid views over the surrounding landscape.

PILL Two views of this small village beside the River Avon, downstream from Bristol, one of which demonstrates the impact of the new bridge carrying M5 traffic out of Somerset to the north and to London. The name of the place (formerly Crockerne Pill) means simply 'creek' and here lived the pilots on whom generations of Bristol seamen relied for safe passage. There was also a ferry here across the river to Shirehampton until 1970. A plaque by the old landing slip claims that John Cabot spent several days here before sailing on to discover North America in 1497. Until 1861 the place always lay within the parish of Easton-in-Gordano, otherwise known as St George's from the dedication of its church, whose village lies further to the west. Apart from its medieval tower, the church was rebuilt in 1872, but in its churchyard lie generations of the inhabitants of Pill, many of whom drowned in the course of their work.

PILTON Two of the many delightful houses and cottages which punctuate the hillside slope of this charming village. The manor formed one of the earliest possessions of Glastonbury Abbey, given by King Ine of the West Saxons in about 700, and the abbots established a substantial house and deer park here. The present Manor House represents the abbots' country retreat, although almost wholly rebuilt since the abbey's dissolution. What survives from Glastonbury's time is a square dovecot and a superb nine-bay barn of about 1375, although sadly without its roof after a lightning strike and fire in 1964. The abbey had vineyards here in 1189, and since 1966 a new and successful vineyard has been created around the Manor. The church of St John the Baptist here received so many gifts of livestock that the parish had to appoint wardens to look after them. In 1794 Thomas Withys was hanged at Stone Gallows, near Taunton, for drowning his wife in a pond at Pilton.

PORLOCK WEIR Picturesque 17th century cottages on the shingle beach, once occupied entirely by fishermen and by those who formerly worked this little port. The weir or harbour here was evidently being built during the 1420s, possibly because access by sea to Porlock itself was then becoming silted up. The present harbour dates from the 19th century, only one merchant vessel seems ever to have been built here (in 1858) and the last coal boat discharged in 1950. Today the place is a popular mooring for yachts, for coastal walks and for a refreshing pint in the old Ship Inn. An epitaph here to Thomas Rawle and Prudence his wife, who died on successive days in 1786, runs:

> *He first departed – she for one day*
> *   tried*
> *To live without him, lik'd it not and*
> *   died.*

PRISTON Surrounded by a green rolling landscape, the situation of this pretty little village was described by Collinson in 1791 as 'on a rising ground in a woody vale'. Indeed, Ekwall interprets its name as 'settlement in a copse or thicket'. Granted to Bath Priory (later Abbey) in 931 by King Athelstan it was retained by the monks until the dissolution of their house in 1539. The central church tower of St Luke, dated 1751 and just visible towards the left of the picture, supports an enormous weathercock which local tradition says was filled with beer (and drained !) before being hoisted into place. There is a Norman nave and south doorway: in the latter a fine studded medieval door. Still grinding near the village is Priston Mill, probably on the same site as its Domesday (1086) precursor, then valued at 7s 6d a year.

PUBLOW A leafy view of the Perpendicular four-stage tower of All Saints church. This was originally a chapelry of the minster or mother church of Keynsham to the north-east, and with that church formed part of the endowment of Keynsham Abbey. That monastery was founded soon after 1166 by William, Earl of Gloucester, lord also of Publow: this place-name meaning 'Pybba's mound' or 'barrow'. Separated from Publow by the River Chew, and the old bridge which spans it, is the more substantial and industrial village of Pensford which formerly straddled the parish boundary between Publow and Stanton Drew.

PURITON The approach to the church of St Michael and All Angels past the triangular village green. The church has a 13th century west tower topped off with a steep pyramidal roof: the rest of the building largely rebuilt in the 15th century. The manor here was held before the Conquest by Queen Edith, wife of Edward the Confessor. Inevitably seized by William I after the Battle of Hastings, Puriton became the only estate in the country which the Conqueror gave to the Pope who had endorsed his English adventure. Later owners included the Greenhill family of Knowle Hall in neighbouring Bawdrip, whose 19th and 20th century monuments fill the north aisle of the church. The most prominent features of the parish are now the Royal Ordnance Factory, built to the east of the village from 1939, and the M 5, cut through the west of the parish in the 1970s. There has been much modern building around the outskirts to house Bridgwater commuters.

QUEEN CAMEL A cat garnishes the church path, lined by these stone cottages whose climbing roses are just coming into bloom. It is a village south-west from Sparkford with an abundance of attractive houses and well-kept gardens. Before the Conquest it was held by Gytha, after whom the village school is named and who was mother to King Harold who died at Hastings. It was known briefly as Camel Regis ('King's Camel') in 1275 but after Edward I gave it to his wife, Eleanor, it adopted its present name. Long held by the Crown, the manor was granted in 1558 to Sir Walter Mildmay, founder of Emmanuel College, Cambridge, and Chancellor of the Exchequer, whose coat of arms still adorn the village inn sign. His descendants settled at Hazelgrove House to the north-west of the village, rebuilding it in the 18th century and finally selling up in 1929. The Mildmay memorials figure prominently in the south aisle of the fine 14th century church of St Bartholomew in the middle of the village.

RIMPTON A thatched medieval cottage in this attractive village to the north-east of Yeovil. The name Rimpton, meaning 'settlement on the border', reflects its position on the boundary with Dorset. In 953 King Eadred granted the manor to Brihtric Grim, under whose will it passed to the bishops of Winchester. They administered Rimpton with their great manor of Taunton Deane and remained its lords until they sold it in 1822. The bishops' accounts document day-to-day life here, including the Christmas feasts they provided for their tenants, with payments for meat, wheat, cheese and malt to make beer. All but the chancel of the church of St Mary was probably built by Bishop Richard Fox of Winchester (1501-28), whose pelican badge appears on an outer parapet.

RODE A street scene in this former clothing village midway between Frome and Trowbridge. The River Frome provided water power for several mills as early as 1086 and cloth manufacture reached its height in the 18th and early 19th centuries, Rocabella Mill being credited with devising the original Royal Blue hue for King George III. Lawrence de St Maur (Seymour) secured a Thursday market and three day fair here in 1283, the latter continuing as Rode Revel into the 19th century. In the 18th century tourists came to take the waters, the end product being marketed in Bath in 1746. Today it is the Tropical Bird Gardens in the former grounds of Rode Manor which draw the visitors. Around the Perpendicular church of St Lawrence, sited at the south-eastern edge of the village, the parishioners used to dance with linked hands every Shrove Tuesday. They ended with a great shout intended to drive the Devil away for the forthcoming year.

SEAVINGTON ST MARY This peaceful lane which runs eastwards down the slope into this little village was until 1829 part of the main road from Ilminster to Ilchester. With its neighbour, Seavington St Michael, the village was named for 'the seven settlements' that in Saxon times lay within their joint boundaries. The manor here was formerly known as Seavington Vaux and Robert Vaux gave Somerset's first recorded windmill here to Montacute Priory in about 1212. Later, from 1876, the place was acquired by the Vaughan Lee family as part of the nearby Dillington estate. The church of St Mary, dating from the 13th century with a porch and west tower built in about 1500, was declared redundant in 1983. It was held as a chapelry of South Petherton by Bruton Priory and, from 1539, by the Dean and Chapter of Bristol Cathedral. Within the parish but closer to Seavington St Michael is the hamlet of Seavington Abbots, granted by King Cnut (Canute) to Athelney Abbey in about 1030.

SEAVINGTON ST MICHAEL The main A 303 through the centre of the village has been a relatively quiet byway since the Ilminster bypass opened in 1988. The Volunteer Inn, set back on the right side of the road in the middle distance, has been ministering to thirsty locals and travellers since at least 1833. The manor was owned by Siward the falconer at the time of Domesday (1086), by 1232 had passed to Adam the Dane, after whom it was known as Seavington Dennis and was subsequently held in turn by Glastonbury Abbey and Winchester College. The church of St Michael lies at the southern edge of the village and has a 12th century nave and 13th century chancel. A manor house mentioned in 1383 probably stood in Court Close, a field immediately west of the church.

SELWORTHY Looking north to this Exmoor village and its prominent parish church, framed by mature woodland with the bare hill slope beyond. One of the most beautiful spots in the county, it owes much of its romantic appeal to the Acland family who inherited the main manor in 1802. The cluster of thatched cottages around Selworthy Green, which feature in our second picture, were built in 1828 by Sir Thomas Dyke Acland for his former servants and he was responsible for planting much of the woodland in the area. In 1944 Sir Thomas's descendant, Sir Richard Acland, transferred his Holnicote estate of over 12,000 acres here to the National Trust. Holnicote itself, long used by the Aclands as their Exmoor retreat and which suffered major fires in 1779, 1851 and 1941, is now a hotel. The whitewashed church of All Saints stands high above the village: entirely Perpendicular apart from its 14th century west tower. The ornate Holnicote south aisle of 1538 was probably the work of Philip Steyning and the whole building is unusually rich in monuments. Below the church is a converted 13th century tithe barn bearing carvings of tithable produce – a pig, a lamb and a wheatsheaf.

SHAPWICK At the north-western end of this village stands Shapwick House Hotel, the E-shaped former manor, the main house (right) being the remodelling of a 15th century house in 1630 by Sir Henry Rolle, who became Lord Chief Justice during the Commonwealth. The clock tower (centre) was added in 1865. Shapwick probably formed the principal settlement on the Polden estate granted to Glastonbury Abbey in 729, its name, 'sheep farm', suggesting an economy based on grazing livestock on the Levels. The village's grid iron plan may derive from a 10th century development by the abbey, which held the place until 1539. The former rectory estate was centred on the medieval Shapwick Manor, remodelled by the Bull family in the early 17th century and now a school. The original St Andrew's church stood near Beerway to the east of the village, succeeded by a new church of St Mary in

the centre of the village, consecrated in 1331, although the present building with central tower is a mix of Decorated and Perpendicular.

SHEPTON BEAUCHAMP This road junction in the middle of the village is still known as the Shambles: recalling the Friday market and the annual fairs founded in 1260 by the lord of the manor, Robert de Beauchamp. The sign of the flower-bedecked Duke of York Inn was moved to the present building in about 1860 from a site south of the school in the main street. The Beauchamps had obtained the manor by the mid 12th century, probably with the barony of Hatch Beauchamp, from whom it descended in 1361 to the Seymours. It is possible that the 6-year-old Jane Seymour, later third wife of Henry VIII, lived here while her father was sheriff of Somerset and occupied the manor house at the south

end of the village. Apart from agriculture, gloving occupied the female population from the early 18th century and gave employment to 139 women here in 1861.

SOUTH CHERITON The former toll
house on the old Vale of Blackmoor
turnpike road between Wincanton and
Templecombe, displaying the tolls in force
in 1824. From this point on the main road
a lane runs east through the village: a
separate manor in 1086 but generally held
with Horsington, within which parish it
lay.

SOUTH STOKE Viewed from the south it is hard to believe that this unspoilt village is only two miles over the hill from Bath to the north. In the centre of the picture stands the church of St James the Great. It has a Norman north doorway, although the west tower is Perpendicular. The rest of the church was rebuilt in 1712 and the chancel again in the 19th century, with the addition of a south aisle in 1845. The manor was restored to Bath Priory by King Edgar in 961, when it was called 'Tottanstoc', 'Totta's (holy ?) place'. The Packhorse Inn, a prominent feature of the village, was built in 1674 as a farmhouse called the Breach, becoming an inn only in 1853. Its predecessor under the same sign is believed to have been the present Packhorse Farm on the old Midford Road. This was apparently the haunt of tea smugglers, two tons of which were carried off from there in 1779 after a violent struggle with Revenue Officers. Manor Farm of about 1670 has an excellent barn and dovecot of about 1500.

SPAXTON Within a compact village in a large parish with several scattered hamlets stands this Quantock cottage with its neatly tended garden, close to the church of St Margaret (formerly dedicated to St Mary). In origin the church was possibly a Saxon minster, for there was a rural deanery here in the later 12th century, although the rectors were later presented by successive lords of the main manor. In matters religious, however, Spaxton is perhaps best known beyond its bounds for the Agapemone or 'Abode of Love', an aberrant sect founded in 1846 by the unfrocked curate of nearby Charlinch, Henry Prince. Designed to attract wealthy single females behind its walls and deprive them of their funds, more in the manner of a modern American religious cult, it continued until 1958 and its buildings survive at Four Forks.

STANTON PRIOR Just east of the A39 from Wells to Bath lies the small village of Stanton Prior, its appealing cottages and farmhouses built, as the first part of its name implies, of stone. In 963 King Edgar granted this manor to his 'decurion' Aelfsige, presumably for life, and again in 965 to Bath Abbey (later Priory), after which the second part of its name was added, the monastery retaining the estate until its dissolution. The church of St Lawrence (centre) has a Perpendicular west tower and 13th century north porch and south doorway: the remainder all dating from a thorough restoration in 1869. There is also an intriguing and elaborate skull-ridden memorial to the family of Thomas Cox (died 1650).

STAPLE FITZPAINE The fine Perpendicular tower of St Peter's church towards the south end of the village beside the road south from Taunton to the Blackdown Hills. The place was formerly known as Staple Briwes after the family that held it by 1200 and of whom Robert de Briwes secured a market, fair and the right to hunt here in 1233, while the Fitzpaines owned the manor between 1307 and 1393. Modern Staple owes its present complexion to the Portmans of nearby Orchard Portman, who bought the manor in 1600 and retained it until 1944. Sir William Portman built the attractive range of almshouses near the church in 1643 and Staple Manor was put up by the martinet minister, the Rev Fitzhardinge Berkeley Portman, as his substantial rectory in 1840. It is, however, the gastronomic attractions of the Greyhound Inn which give Staple its modern magnetism.

STOCKLINCH Two of the delightful thatched cottages that typify this secluded village to the north-east of Ilminster. In fact it was formerly two villages that over the centuries have grown together. The larger of these, Stocklinch Magdalene, takes its suffix from the dedication of the small church of St Mary Magdalene and from 1426 the manor formed the endowment of Robert Veel's Ilchester almshouses. The second village, Stocklinch Ottersey, derived its name from its ownership by the king's hawker (*otricer*) from the late 12th century. The church of St Mary, redundant since 1973 and dating from the 13th century, stands isolated above the village on the hillside and can only be reached on foot – a walk that is well worth the effort. Monuments to the Jeffrey(s) lords of the manor dating from the 17th century led to the unfounded tradition that the unrelated and notorious Judge Jeffreys was secretly buried here.

STOFORD The 16th century former Guildhall at Stoford, a village in the parish of Barwick to the south of Yeovil. Named for the one-time 'stone ford' across the River Yeo at this point, the crossing is now marked by a two-arched bridge. A borough was established here by William de Cantilupe, whose family gave Chilton Cantelo its suffix, probably around the period that he secured a fair (1228) and market (1231) for his new creation. There were 74 burgages here in 1272 and an earlier Guildhall ('Zuldhous') was recorded in 1353. The portreeve and officers were still walking in procession on fair days in 1633 but, although a second fair was obtained in 1671, the growth of Yeovil put paid to its commercial prospects. Stoford remains, however, a delightful group of cottages fronting the village green and former market place.

STOGUMBER A distant view of the village from its harvested hinterland. The red sandstone church of St Mary, possibly a Saxon minster in origin, stands above the village. It was largely rebuilt in the 15th century although the base of the tower and part of the south aisle survive from an earlier building of about 1300. In the south aisle stands the ornate memorial to Sir George Sydenham (died 1589), builder of nearby Combe Sydenham Hall, whose daughter Elizabeth married the Elizabethan seafarer, Sir Francis Drake, at Monksilver in 1583. North of the church is the former market place, where by 1614 the Sydenhams were holding a market which continued until the 19th century. The market hall with assembly room over of about 1800 is now incorporated in the White Horse Inn (recorded in 1748). In 1784 the same market place was the chosen location for an unusual transaction, when miller William Bacon sold his wife and four children to labourer Robert Jones for 5s (25p)!

STOKE PERO Looking down from Wilmersham on this remote and isolated little Exmoor hamlet. Today there is little there apart from the tiny church and the adjacent Church Farm and outbuildings, although in 1791 there were as many as 14 houses near the church. The Pirou family (named from Pirou in Normandy), from whom Stoke derives the second part of its name, held an estate here between the 12th and 14th centuries and may have built the first church. The present church has a 13th century saddleback tower but the body of the building was almost wholly rebuilt by Sir Charles Thomas Dyke Acland in 1897, and one donkey called Zulu is credited with hauling all the necessary timber up from Porlock. Poignantly, even in this remote parish the Black Death carried off three successive rectors in 1348-9.

TICKENHAM The church of SS Quiricus and Julietta (4th century martyred mother and son) standing with Tickenham Court upon a rise and almost surrounded by moors in which St Mark's Hospital, Bristol, was granted the right to dig peat in the mid 13th century. From this point a lane leads north to the main village which lines the B 3130 from Clevedon to Nailsea. The church of 'Tica's settlement' has a nave, chancel and chancel arch built within 40 years of the Norman Conquest. To these were added a south chancel chapel and side aisles in the early 13th century, and later, in Perpendicular style, the west tower and various windows. There are three 13th century effigies, some 14th century stained glass in the south chapel and a font of about 1300. Tickenham Court has a remarkably intact medieval hall and a solar wing of about 1500 added to it: probably the work of the FitzNicholas family and their descendants, the Poyntzes.

TINTINHULL A peaceful intersection in this Hamstone village south-west from Ilchester, marked by Tintinhull Court (left). This house was the medieval rectory until Montacute Priory, which had held both church and manor since 1102, ordained a vicarage in 1529. Thereafter it became a private house, acquired by the Napper family who largely rebuilt it in the 17th and 18th centuries. The Nappers took a lease of the manor in 1628 and bought it from Francis Petre in 1673. They were also responsible for upgrading the present Tintinhull House for a younger brother, Andrew Napper, in the early 18th century, the family retaining it until 1835. Its gardens, developed by noted botanist, Dr Price, from 1898 and by Mrs Reiss from 1933, have been National Trust property since 1954. The church of St Margaret dates from the early 13th century but was later remodelled in Perpendicular style. The south porch can be dated to 1441-2, the benchends to 1511-12 and a churchyard gate or 'stonyng door' put up by the prior of Montacute in 1517.

UBLEY A distant view of this delightful village, 'Ubba's glade', sited below the Mendips between Chew Valley and Blagdon lakes, with a close-up of its small village green, cross and strident telephone box. The cross (rebuilt 1901) probably indicates the site of the Monday market and St Bartholomew's fair obtained by Richard D'Amory in the 14th century. The 13th century church of St Bartholomew (whence the date of the fair) was remodelled in Perpendicular style with the addition of side aisles. Edmund Dirrick, parish clerk here, used the parish register to record the effects on Ubley of the terrible 13-week frost of 1683-4, the storm of 1703 which unroofed houses, uprooted trees and ruined crops, and the drought of 1709 which killed livestock and drove up the price of produce to horrendous levels. Today, apart from agriculture, the village's economy rests on its sawmills and a flourishing trout hatchery.

WAYFORD A quiet lane in this former satellite of Crewkerne: its church once a chapelry whose key was annually laid on the altar of Crewkerne church until 1833-4 in token of its subservience. The principal estate, evidently created from Crewkerne manor soon after the compilation of the Domesday Book in 1086, was held by William of Wayford by 1200 and thereafter passed by marriage through a succession of families to the Daubeneys in the early 16th century. Although the estate was split up and sold from 1627 onwards, Wayford Manor, beside the church, was retained by Daubeney descendants until 1700, including Dr Daubeney Turberville (1612-96), a famous oculist consulted by Samuel Pepys and Princess Anne and who founded a charity for the poor of the parish.

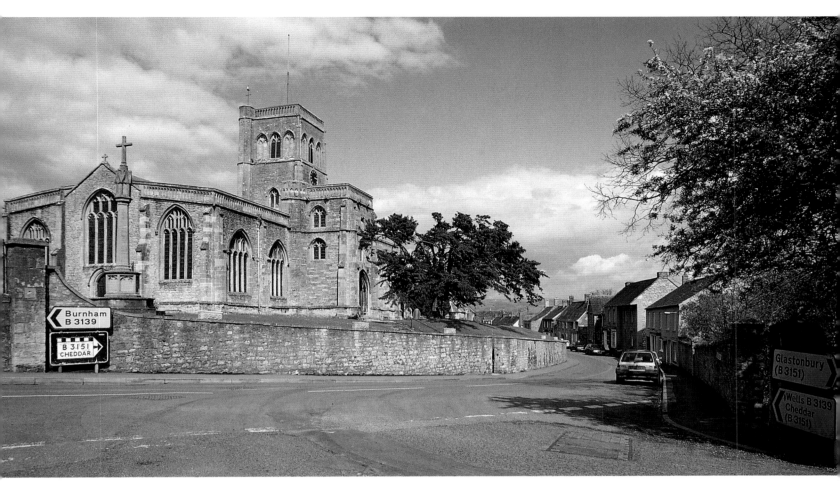

WEDMORE The major Perpendicular church of St Mary Magdalene, rival to that of North Curry for the title 'Cathedral of the Moors' (as the Levels are often known) rises above the centre of the village. Indeed the wealth of the place depended on the extensive grazing land throughout this large parish. Here in 878 King Alfred brought the Danish king Guthrum to conclude the Treaty of Wedmore after the Battle of Edington, which freed the kingdom of the West Saxons from the pillaging of the Vikings. The deans of Wells Cathedral, lords of the manor by 1157, established a borough here in the 13th century, ruled by a portreeve as late as 1791. A three-day fair around the church's dedication day and a Tuesday market were established in 1255 and the borough court annually appointed bread weighers, ale tasters, haywards, water bailiffs and constables. In 1857 John Bunn of Wedmore was proclaimed backsword (cudgel-playing) champion of England after a contest in Berkshire.

WELLOW Attractive stone houses in the main street of this village, south from Bath, its name being derived from a British stream name, recorded as 'Welwe' in 766 and possibly meaning 'winding'. This same Wellow Brook is crossed here by a picturesque packhorse bridge and ford. The substantial church of St Julian seems uniformly of the later 14th century, apart from a discreetly rebuilt chancel of 1890, and the building is well furnished with font of about 1300, rood screen, early benchends, wallpaintings in the (north) Hungerford chapel and several good memorials, including a priest's effigy of 1400. At Wellow was born Dr John Bull (1563-1628), celebrated organist and choirmaster at London and Antwerp, whom some hail as the original composer of our National Anthem.

WEST BAGBOROUGH A happy
juxtaposition of Quantock church and
manor house, looking down over the Vale
of Taunton. The Perpendicular church of
St Pancras was heavily restored by the
Victorians and a north aisle added in
1839. A notable compensation is the
modern carving by Sir Ninian Comper
and memorials and heraldic hatchments
of the Popham (later Brooke-Popham)
family, who live here and have owned the
manor from the early 18th century. They
rebuilt Bagborough House with its
colonnade in a simple but enchanting
parkland setting. The village below has a
goodly number of thatched cottages
strung out along a single lane. In this
parish in 1949 one traditional remedy
recommended that cattle lice should be
spread between bread and butter and
given to the patient. 'Afterwards tell him
what he ate. He may be sick but he'll
never have jaundice' !

WEST CAMEL One of Somerset's few thatched post offices which stands in the centre of the village: built like so many of the houses in that area of the golden stone from Ham Hill. The manor here was sometimes known as Camel Abbatis after its situation near Camel Hill and its tenure from the 10th century by Muchelney Abbey – from which period part of a Saxon cross-shaft survives in the parish church. It was an estate that was always dependent on agriculture (there is a fine tithe barn of about 1500 near the medieval rectory) although four dyers polluted the river here in 1436. The patronage of the rectory was acquired from Muchelney by Bishop Jocelin in 1239, which led to the parish generally being served over the centuries by absentee officers and relatives of successive bishops.

WESTON BAMPFYLDE The lane leading past attractive grey stone cottages to the church of the Holy Cross, south from Sparkford. The base of the tower is 13th century with a Perpendicular octagonal top and inside is a Norman font and Jacobean pulpit. A monument inside commemorates the wife of Nathaniel Mist, 18th century radical printer and friend of Daniel Defoe. The manor house to the east of the church was held by the Bampfyldes from 1316 until recently, the present building dating from the 17th century.

WHITELACKINGTON Thatched cottage and kitchen garden in this small village to the east of Ilminster, bisected by the old A 38 but blessed with a new peace since the Ilminster bypass opened in 1988. The manor, which in 1086 sustained seven swineherds paying their rent in kind (40 pigs), was held by the Speke family from 1430 until 1795. In the grounds of the 16th and 17th century manor house beside the church the Duke of Monmouth was entertained by George Speke beneath a giant chestnut tree in 1680. Five years later the Duke's rebellion led to the hanging, drawing and quartering of Charles Speke in Ilminster market place: guilty only of shaking Monmouth's hand. It was Charles's brother John who rode out with the rebels but, as he had escaped, Judge Jeffreys decided that the family owed the king a life. The church of St Mary has 14th century transepts but the rest was rebuilt in Perpendicular style. It contains two medieval effigies and an Elizabethan monument to former lords of the place.

WHITESTAUNTON In the extreme south of the county where the Blackdown Hills slope east towards Chard, this small village lies in the valley beside the parish church, at the gates of the substantial manor house and adjoining St Agnes' Well and the site of a Roman villa. The estate here, held by the Saxon Alward before the Norman Conquest, passed to Ansgar Brito after it, descending with Ansgar's barony of Odcombe. The rambling Whitestaunton Manor, almost hidden behind trees in the picture, dates from the later 15th century: a simple small manor house almost encapsulated by subsequent Tudor and Stuart extensions. The builder was probably John Brett (died 1478), heir of the Stauntons, who had taken their name from the manor and held it since at least 1166. The Bretts were notorious Roman Catholics after the Reformation and the house became a nursery for prominent Jesuits: the village a local refuge from persecution for Roman Catholic recusants. Bought from the Bretts by Sir Abraham Elton of Bristol in 1718, the manor continued in a junior branch of his family until 1925.

WINSFORD My favourite Exmoor village which lies to the north of Dulverton in a steep-sided valley at the junction of six early lanes. Surrounded by wooded hills, the place has a charming village green and seven small stone bridges which criss-cross the Winn Brook and the River Exe. The manor was held before 1066 by Tostig, brother of King Harold II, but, like so much of Exmoor, eventually passed into the hands of the Acland family. The church of St Mary Magdalene stands above the village and is mainly Perpendicular apart from the 13th century chancel and Norman south doorway. Near the thatched Royal Oak Hotel a plaque identifies the birthplace of Ernest Bevin, Foreign Secretary, born in 1881 the illegitimate son of Dianna Bevin, probably by local butcher, William Pearse.

WINSHAM Looking towards the junction of five roads at the northern end of the village, marked by a village green and the remains of a medieval cross. Here were probably held both the market and fair secured in 1262 by the canons of Wells Cathedral. The manor had been held by the cathedral from Saxon times and, although seized by King Harold II, was restored after the Battle of Hastings. The church of St Stephen with central tower stands halfway down the main street. Although its basic structure may well be Norman, there are Decorated details and the building was clearly remodelled in Perpendicular style. On the inner north wall of the tower hangs an impressive 16th century painting of the Crucifixion and there are several monuments to the Henley family of Leigh House, an E-shaped mansion to the west of the village.

WITHYPOOL The bridge spanning the River Barle which joins Pennycombe Water at this Exmoor village. Formerly an even more remote place, it used to be said of Withypool that there were four harvests a year here – snow, frost, rain and muck ! A little further upstream from the village another crossing, Lanacre Bridge, marked the open-air meeting place of one of the two annual Swainmote courts which administered Exmoor from medieval times, and the manor was long held with the Forestership of the moor. The church of St Andrew was formerly a chapelry of Hawkridge (in whose churchyard the other Swainmote court met) but was almost entirely restored and rebuilt in 1887 and 1902: only the short 17th century west tower and Norman font being spared.

WOOKEY The spectacular castellated Mellifont Abbey, built in the early 19th century beside the church of St Matthew on the site of the former rectory. The building incorporates medieval fragments believed to have been brought from nearby Court Farm, which was from about 1205 a moated palace of the bishops of Wells, who held the manor here from the foundation of the cathedral in 909 until forced to surrender it to the Duke of Somerset in 1548. The name of the house is supposed to have been borrowed from the original Mellifont Abbey near Drogheda in Ireland by Lady Elizabeth Bertie (died 1781). The church dates from the 14th and 15th centuries and contains an elaborate monument to Thomas Clerke (died 1556), brother of Bishop Clerke, to whom the Wookey estate was leased in 1544.

WOOLAVINGTON The road leading towards the centre of this attractive village to the north-east of Bridgwater at the west end of the Polden Hills. The west tower of the church of St Peter can be seen above the roof lines and appears to have been a former crossing tower of about 1300 to which, when the body of its church was demolished, a Perpendicular nave and chancel were added. A monogrammed stone is thought to commemorate Lord Chief Justice John Hody, who requested burial here in 1441. The church was given by Robert de Chandos to Goldcliff Priory in Monmouthshire in the early 12th century, and to the canons of Windsor in the 15th century. William Pym of Woolavington fell out with his wife, who refused to recognize their marriage, and by his will of 1608 left her £10 'to buy her a great horse, for I could not these many years please her with one great enough'.

WRINGTON Cheerful whitewashed and pastel houses in this former market town. The name means 'settlement on the River Wring', an old stream name for the River Yeo. At the Golden Lion (right) in 1780 the men of Somerset challenged 'the rest of the world' to meet them at cudgel-playing. The manor was granted to Glastonbury Abbey by the ealdorman Athelstan when he became a monk there in the 10th century, and remained the property of the abbey until its dissolution in 1539. The abbot secured the grant of a market and fair in 1332 and the place became a successful trading community. The church of All Saints, whose tower (113 ft) is visible to the left of our picture, has a chancel that dates from 1300 although the rest of the building is 15th century Perpendicular. Memorials include the effigy of a priest (in about 1340) and 19th century busts to Wrington's two most celebrated worthies. John Locke, the radical philosopher and supporter of the Duke of Monmouth, was born in a cottage near the church in 1632, and Hannah More, bluestocking playwright, founder of schools and philanthropist, lived in the parish at Cowslip Green and Barley Wood, and, after her death at Clifton in 1833, was buried with her sisters in the churchyard here. In 1791 she organized an early Sunday school treat by taking 517 children and 300 others from Wrington up to Callow Hill on the Mendips and feasting them in front of 4,000 spectators for a total cost of £15.